THE URBAN SLANG INDEX
STREET TERMINOLOGY DECODED

written by Gwenton Sloley

THE URBAN SLANG INDEX
STREET TERMINOLOGY DECODED

Originally published in Great Britain by Gwenton Sloley in 2014

Copyright © Gwenton Sloley 2014

The right of Gwenton Sloley to be identified as the author of this work has been asserted in accordance with sections 77 and 78 of the copyright Designs and Patents Act 1988.

This book is an autobiography. Places and people mentioned are true to the Authors recollection. Some people's names have been changed for confidentially reasons.

Condition of sale

This book is sold subject to the condition that is shall not, by way of trade or otherwise, be lent, re-sold, hired out or otherwise circulated in any form of binding or cover other than that in which it is published and without a similar condition including this condition being imposed on the subsequent purchaser.

Author: Gwenton Sloley
Phototypeset: Turae, Eon Graphics Ltd
Proof reading and critique: Conscious Smith
Copy editor: James Davies
ISBN: 978-1-291-86882-1
gwenton.sloley@yahoo.com

INTRODUCTION

The roots of London's modern street slang are hard to pinpoint, as the city is a linguistic melting pot of the many races that have left their mark on the capital's language. Traditional "Bow Bells" Cockney English, West Indian patois, Indian and Bangladeshi have all gone to produce Multicultural London English, the academic term for the modern street slang which is spoken from Harlesden to Hackney and from Streatham to Stoke Newington.

I Have worked in the housing sector as a specialist in relation to the housing of ex offenders, vulnerable young people and their families for 10 years. During that time I have also been very involved in the professional development of professionals in related sectors through the training I provide, and the books I write. I have made a point of remaining rooted in the communities I serve that raised me, which I believe has greatly contributed to the efficacy of my work.

Many phrases were used universally - for example LOL (Laugh Out Loud) - and for that you can probably blame rap music, text messaging, Facebook and popular TV programmes like Skins and Hollyoaks.

LONDON STREETS SLANG

Tosser – Idiot
Cock-up – Screw up
Bloody – Damn
Give You A Bell – Call you
Blimey! – My Goodness
Wanker – Idiot
Gutted – Devastated
Bespoke – Custom Made
Chuffed – Proud
Fancy – Like
Sod Off – Piss off
Lost the Plot – Gone Crazy
Fortnight – Two Weeks
Sorted – Arranged
Hoover – Vacuum
Kip – Sleep or nap
Bee's Knees – Awesome
Know Your Onions – Knowledgeable
Dodgy – Suspicious
Wonky – Not right
Wicked – Cool!
Whinge – Whine
Tad – Little bit
Tenner – £10
Fiver – £5
Skive – Lazy or avoid doing something
Toff – Upper Class Person
Punter – Customer/Prostitute's Client
Scouser – Someone from Liverpool
Quid – £
Taking the Piss – Screwing around32. **Pissed** – Drunk
Loo – Toilet
Nicked – Stolen
Nutter – Crazy Person
Knackered – Tired
Gobsmacked – Amazed
Dog's Bollocks – Awesome
Chap – Male or friend
Bugger – Jerk
Bog Roll – Toilet Paper

Bob's Your Uncle – There you go!
Anti-Clockwise – We Say Counter Clockwise
C of E – Church of England
Pants – Panties
Throw a Spanner in the Works – Screw up
Zed – We say ZZZZZZZ
Absobloodylootely – YES!
Nosh – Food
One Off – One time only
Shambles – Mess
Arse-over-tit – Fall over
Brilliant! – Great!
Dog's Dinner – Dressed Nicely
Up for it – Willing to have sex
On the Pull – Looking for sex
Made Redundant – Fired from a job
Easy Peasy – Easy
See a Man About a Dog – Do a deal or take a dump
Up the Duff – Pregnant
DIY – Do It Yourself home improvements
Chat Up – Flirt
Fit – Hot
Arse – Ass
Strawberry Creams – Breasts
Shag – Screw
Gentleman Sausage – Penis
Twigs & Berries – Genitalia
Fanny – Vagina
Bollocks – Balls
Ponce – Poser
Don't Get Your Knickers in a Twist – Don't Get worked up
The Telly – Television
Bangers – Sausage
Chips – French Fries
Daft Cow – Idiot
Do – Party
Uni – College/University
Starkers – Naked
Smeg – From Red Dwarf
Bits 'n Bobs – Various things
Anorak – A person weirdly interested in something
Shambles – bad shape/plan gone wrong
I'm Off to Bedfordshire – Going to bed
Her Majesty's Pleasure – To be in prison
Horses for Courses – Won't work for someone else

John Thomas – Penis
Plastered – Drunk
Meat and Two Veg – Genitalia
Knob Head – Idiot/Dickhead
Knob – Penis
Chav – White trash
It`s monkeys outside – it is very cold
Stag Night – Bachelor Party
Ace – Cool!
Plonker – Idiot
Dobber – Penis
BellEnd – Penis
Blighty – Britain
Bang — punch
Bare — a lot
Bate — obvious
Blud — friend
Booky — suspicious
Butters — ugly
Chug — good-looking
Dutty — nasty
Fam — friends
Gallis — womaniser
Gased — talking nonsense
Gem — fool
Ghost — to be frequently absent
Greezy — bad
Junge — whore
Liccle — small
Marga — extremely skinny
Moist — no ratings, silly, naff
Murk — attack
Nang — good
Peak — used to highlight an eventful situation
Peng — good-looking
Shank — stab
Shower — cool, good
Skadoosh — goodbye
Skettel — loose woman
Slipping — to be caught off-guard
Swag — crap
Tekkers — technique
Wallad — idiot
Wavey — high or drunk

A8 Ball- 3.5 grams of drugs- *"I just picked up an A8 ball"*
AQ - 7.0 grams of drugs quarter
A9 - 9 Ounces
Alie- synonym for innit (I agree)
Allow bredding – to allow copying, to allow cheating
Allow me/ Allow it– *"Leave me alone"* –*"stop it"*
Amp from the word Amplify – to increase ,extend or become more hyper
Arms - to be really strong- -trouble don't want no arms
Bag - £1000- *its going to cost me a "bag"*
Baggamanz (or bag) – Lots, as in *"a bag of people"*
Bait – You are obvious, or simple. As in, *"You're bait blud"*
Bangin – sick/ good *"that girls body is banging"*
Bare – a lot of, very. *"the Queen got bare money"*
Bars – a rap song, part of a song, as in *"spit some bars"*
Baiding – rich, financially stable, solvent. *"you know the queen is baiding"*
Bad – an adjective to describe something that's really cool. *"Them glasses are bad"*
Beef – a hostile disagreement that may result in violence. I don't need *"no beef/ no trouble"*.
Bennin – to be in a state of extreme laughter. *"that comedy show had me bennin"*
Big Mac – Mac 10 –a gun, a weapon
Bing – Prison- been in the bing for two years.
Bobby Brown – Heroine,jus licked a shot of bobby brown.
Burner – Gun *"I need to get a burner"*
Bredrin from the origin (Brethen)- Oringinal meaning brother- also slang for friend *" jus going to check my bredrin"*

Charley – Pure cocaine
Chief – An unintelligent person Fool, or stupid *" your such a chief"* like saying your *"so stupid"*.
Chirps – chat up; talk to *"we chirps some buff gals last night."*
Criss – good, sharp, new. almost onomatoepaeic as in 'crisp'. *"that car iis criss"*
Chung – extremely good looking. If someone is described as "chung", that's better-looking than their "buff" friend. *"that girl is chung"*
Cat- Drug Thene, A person that is addicted to drugs *" jus licked a shot to a cat"*
Chirpsing – Flirtinging, sweet talking *" look at my man chirpsing that ting over there"*.
Clappin' – out of date or worn out, usually to describe attire or accessories, as in *"man, my tracksuit is clappin'. Gotta get down JJB Sport and buy a new one."* Also means tired out.

Cotch – to hang out, relax, chill out or sleep. Possibly derived, via patois, from the French *"se coucher"*, meaning to lie down. See also kotch.
Crepes – trainers: *"check out my new crepe."*
Crump – A multi-purpose term which can be an insult, an exclamation and some other things as well. It generally means bad, but can also mean good, depending on the context: *"that ain't good man, it's crump"* or *"that's one crump message you left there"*.
Chapping- Cold, Freezing *"outside is chapping fam"*
Crutterz- Mashed up, worn out *"That car is crutterz"*
Dash – To dash is to pass something to somebody – but it can be *"pass"* in the broadest possible sense, including to throw violently with the intention of causing hurt or damage.
Dred from the word (Dreadful) – dreadful, terrible, bad,cruel. *"Look at that girl her hair looks dread"*
Drum – Home, *"Im just on my way to my drum"*
Dry- dull, boring, unfunny. A bad joke might be described as *"dry"*.
Endz - Area, neighbourhood *"what endz you from?"*
Extra - Over the top, too much *"you too Extra"*
Fam – Short for Family, friends *"init tho fam"* a word used to refere to finds and fam.
Feds – police. *"Feds stopped me today fam"*
Flat roofin' – to be overworked and stressed, as in *"I was flat roofin for my GCSEs"*. Probably comes from flat out.
Food – Drugs *"have you got any food?"* *"whos got food?"*
From ends- one who is *"from the streets"* or from our area, so knows what's going on. *"his from ends bruv lowe him"*
Garms from the original word (Garments) meaning - clothing. *" I went shopping today bought some new garms"*
(Gas/Gassing/ Gassed)- to talk gas *"shit"* – his gassing *"lying"* shes gassed *"excited"*
Ginuls/jinels – *fixed up or conned by someone/something, or, used to describe something that is a con:" dem phones 4 u deals are a jinels"*. Also to *"bump"*.
Giving air – Ignoring someone, *"been trying to call Joe his airing my calls"*
Grimy - Good, or may describe a practical joke or amusing act.
Gyaldem – a group of *"girls"*
Heads - People (i.e. Bare heads means lots of people)
Hoody- item of clothing ie- *"hooded jumper"*
Hype - Too much. Hyping means acting in a way that's over the top.
Hubz (or Hubby)- Boyfriend the main guy, *"the one your serious about"*
Hench – Musclar *" im gonna start going gym to get hench"*
Hectic – Good, too much *"that new car is hetic"*
In-it (Innit) – Short for "isn't it", often put at the end of sentences for effect

Is-it – As in really?
Inner - Describes someone who is too nosey *"you to inner"- stop being inner"*
Jack - To take, as in *"He jacked my food."*
Jack jones- on your own *"rolling on my jack jones"*
Jam/ Jamming – Relax, relaxing *"juus jamming at yard for now"*
Jokes - funny or enjoyable, as in *"that party was jokes".*
Key - 1.020 Kilograms *"I gotta go pick up a key of food later"*
Kotch - sit and chill out. See also cotch.
Line - Drug phone- *" I got bare cats on my line"*
Link - to meet someone, to hook up with them, also Woman/Man on the side
Lips/Lipsing - to kiss or kissing
Lip/ Lippy - rude or mouthy *"that girl was getting lippy"*
Long - a task that involves more effort than the object is worth. To be complex, time consuming or arduous in nature
Lush - good-looking *" her outfit is so luch"*
Mandem – A good friend, in a group of boys.
Manz – Refers to oneself *" manz like me"*
Mash – A firearm, gun
Mashing – having Intercourse
Marvin from the word (Starvin) – Hungry
Merk – This word originally meant to kill someone, but now it means to insult someone.
Militant – Meaning stern, difficult or hard
Nang - Good
Next man – Someone who isn't involved, a random person
Nose – Pure cocaine
Not bothered- Someone who is not interested in something, or in doing Something *I don't care what happens to my life to be real with you I'm not bothered.*
On top – when a situation is out of control *this beef is on top if they see me Im dead..*
Off the hook – cool, appealing, fresh, *"That rave was off the hook it ended too soon".*
Older – an older kid who has your back *no one cant touch me cause his my older.*
Owned - to be made a fool of. *"That kid is my worker I own him".*
Pagon – enemy *"I don't like them boys they are pagon"s.*
Pen – (Prison) *I done 2 years in the pen." Been in pen for 2 years"*
Peng – (Good looking) *"That girl is peng".*
Po-po – (Police) *"run the po-po are coming".*

Reh teh teh – Etc, etc
Ringers - stolen car/ bike wipe different number plates *"jus got some ringers to shot"*
Rinsed - overused, used up, all gone. "That song was rinsed, I don't like it anymore."
Roll with – *"im about to roll out"* as in go out
Rude boy(or rudeboi) – a badman, a person who is hardened by the Street. *"don't mess with him his a rude boi"*
Safe – cool, good, sweet. *"safe for that ting fam"* another word for thanks
Safe House - House where drugs/guns are kept
Seckle - Settle down, as in *"calm down or chill"*
Shabby (the opposite of the actual meaning) raggaded – cool, smart, *"da bomb"*. *That car is shabby how much it cost.*
Shook – nervous, scared *"the other gang got you shook that's why you never going into their area".*
Shank – (Knife) *"did you hear about that boy that got shanked last night".*
Shot – (to sell) *"I just licked a shot to that cat stella".*
Sick – interesting, cool, *"That new phone you got is sick I want one".*
Slipping – (Cuaght off Guard) *"I got stabbed because they caught me slipping in their area"*
Skeen – (I see) ooh *skeen*
Squalay – (To leave) *"I'm gonna squalay from my girl once I get back to London".*
Standard – (Goes without saying); *Johns my boy and were all about this road life standard*
Swag/ swagger – (style) how you wear your clothing, *"I like that guys swagger"*
Switch- (To turn on someone) *"He just switch and started rolling with the other gang his a trator".*
Taxed – (to take) *"you got taxed" you gotta pay up to sell drugs on my patch".*
Teefing – (Stealing) *your not a robber man you just a teeth.*
Teeth – Bullets *don't use out all the teeth with your wild shooting its £5 for one.*
Ticked – (Not payed for) *could you tick me £20 till Friday when I get paid I will pay you back.*
Tight – (Mean) *your so tight you never want to spend your money.*
Ting – (can refere too different things) *go get the ting and meet me in the car.*
Tingsing – To flirt or hit on *that woman was try to tingsing me last night.*
Tonks – (Muscular or big people) *you think your all tonks now cause your going gym.*
Tourist – (A clueless person) *your just a tourist you get lost every where.*
Treck – (journey far away) *that party is a treck if were not getting a taxi home im not going.*
Trident – (Armed police) *were not feeling them trident police they don't play around.*
Tune – (Your favourite song) *"that's my tune on the radio"*

Two twos –(next minute) I was waiting for my friend when two twos some dog started chasing us"

Vexed –(Angry), upset *Don't get me vex cause I will hurt you.*
wah'gwan – short for 'what's goin onn', *Wha'gwan brother you good.*
Wettin – (Running) "I was wetting it down the road to get home"
Watch – Be careful; *dont mess with me cause you will have to watch yourself.*
Wicked – cool *that jacket is wicked where you buy it I want one.*
Wifey – Girlfriend *you're my main girl I love you.*
Whip– (car) "jumped in my whip"
Whitney - Crack cocaine
Yard - house,(where one lives and hangs out).
Younger – (Sibling), someone younger than you; someone you protect
Zoot – (a splif)or a roll-up *wich contains weed.* "roll me a zoot"

COCKNEY SLANG

Adam and Eve – believe
Alan Whickers – knicker
Apples and Pears – stairs
Artful Dodger – lodger
Ascot Races – braces
Aunt Joanna – piano
Baked Bean – Queen
Baker's Dozen – Cousin
Ball and Chalk – Walk
Barnaby Rudge – Judge
Barnet Fair – hair
Barney Rubble – trouble
Battlecruiser – boozer
bees and honey – money
bird lime – time (in prison)
Boat Race – face
Bob Hope – soap
Bottle and glass – arse
Brahms and Liszt – pissed (drunk)
Brass Tacks – facts
Bread and Cheese – sneeze
Bread and Honey – money
Bricks and Mortar – daughter
Bristol City – breasts
Brown Bread – dead
Bubble and Squeak – Greek
Bubble Bath – Laugh
butcher's hook – a look
Chalfont St. Giles – piles
Chalk Farm – arm
china plate – mate (friend)
Cock and Hen – ten
Cows and Kisses – Missus (wife)
Currant bun – sun (also The Sun, a British newspaper)

Custard and jelly – telly (television)
Daisy Roots – boots
Darby and Joan – moan
Dicky bird – word

Dicky Dirt – shirt
Dinky Doos – shoes
Dog and bone – phone
Dog's meat – feet [from early 20th c.]
Duck and Dive – skive
Duke of Kent – rent
Dustbin lid – kid
Elephant's Trunk – drunk
Fireman's Hose – nose
Flowery Dell – cell
Frog and Toad – road
Gypsy's kiss – piss
Half-inch – pinch (to steal)
Hampton Wick – prick
Hank Marvin – starving
Irish Pig – wig
Isle of Wight – tights
Jam-Jar – car
Jimmy Riddle – piddle
Joanna – piano (pronounced 'pianna' in Cockney)
Khyber Pass – arse
Kick and Prance – dance
Lady Godiva – fiver
Laugh n a joke – smoke
Lionel Blairs – flares
Loaf of Bread – head
loop the loop – soup
Mickey Bliss – piss
Mince Pies – eyes
Mork and Mindy – windy'
North and south – mouth
Orchestra stalls – balls
Pat and Mick – sick
Peckham Rye – tie
Plates of meat – feet
Pony and Trap – crap
raspberry ripple – nipple
raspberry tart – fart
Roast Pork – fork
Rosy Lee – tea (drink)
Round the Houses – trousers
Rub-a-Dub – pub
Ruby Murray – curry

Any road: used in place of "any way," primarily used in the north of Britain.

Baccy: shortened word for "tobacco;" also, "wacky backy" means marijuana.

Barmy: crazy, insane; always derogatory.

Bender: derogatory term for homosexual, like "poof." (Note: You probably shouldn't use it or you'll get slapped, but it's worthy of note for giving *Futurama* a very different meaning.)

Biggie: term children might use to describe feces; also, an erection.

Bits 'n Bobs: various things. (Example: "My mother has a lot of Bits 'n Bobs around the house.")

"Bob's your uncle!": "There you go! You've got it!"

Bollocks: technically means "balls," but often describes something seen as extremely negative or lacking in value; e.g. "total shit."

"Bugger off!": "Go away!" or "Leave me alone!" (Note: Bugger, used on its own, is akin to "Fuck!" or "Shit!")

Chav: way young people dress in Essex or southend.

Cheeky: to be not respectful of something, having a flippant or facetious attitude.

Chin Wag: to have a chat with someone.

Collywobbles: extreme queasiness or stomach pain brought on by stress, nervousness or anxiety.

Crusty Dragon: a piece of snot or booger.

Daft Cow: a very stupid person (See also: "Wazzock.")

Dog's Bollocks: extremely good or favorable, great

Dog's Dinner: to be dressed nicely or look dapper.

Donkey's Years: ages, as in "I haven't seen you in ages!"

Fagged: disturbed, bothered or interrupted (Example: If one were studying for a test, one would not want to be "fagged.")

Fall Arse Over Tit: to have an embarrassing fall or to topple over.

Fanny: vagina.

Fit: hot or sexually desirable.

The Full Monty: going all the way with it, going big instead of going home.

"Get stuffed!": "Beat it" or "Scram!"

Gobby: loudly opinionated, offensive or prickish. (See: Donald Trump.)

Gobsmacked: amazed or awed by something.

Gormless: completely clueless, like Alicia Silverstone in the 90s film.

To Have A Butcher's: to take a look at something or someone.

Her Majesty's Pleasure: being incarcerated or put in prison.

"How's Your Father?": euphemism for sex (Example: "Have you and your wife had any of the ol' 'How's your father?' recently?")

"I'm Off To Bedfordshire!": "I'm hitting the hay!"

"It's Monkeys Outside!": "Wow, it's very cold out!"

John Thomas: penis.

Knackered: phrase meaning "extremely tired," often uttered after a long, exhausting day; also see: "zonked."

Knees Up: A term for a mixer or a dance party (Example: "I went to this wild knees up this weekend. I wish you could have been there.")

Legless: totally, completely hammered.

Lose The Plot: to go "crazy" or become mentally unstable.

Lurgy: sick or under the weather.

Made Redundant: to be fired or let go from one's position.

Minted: to be extremely rich.

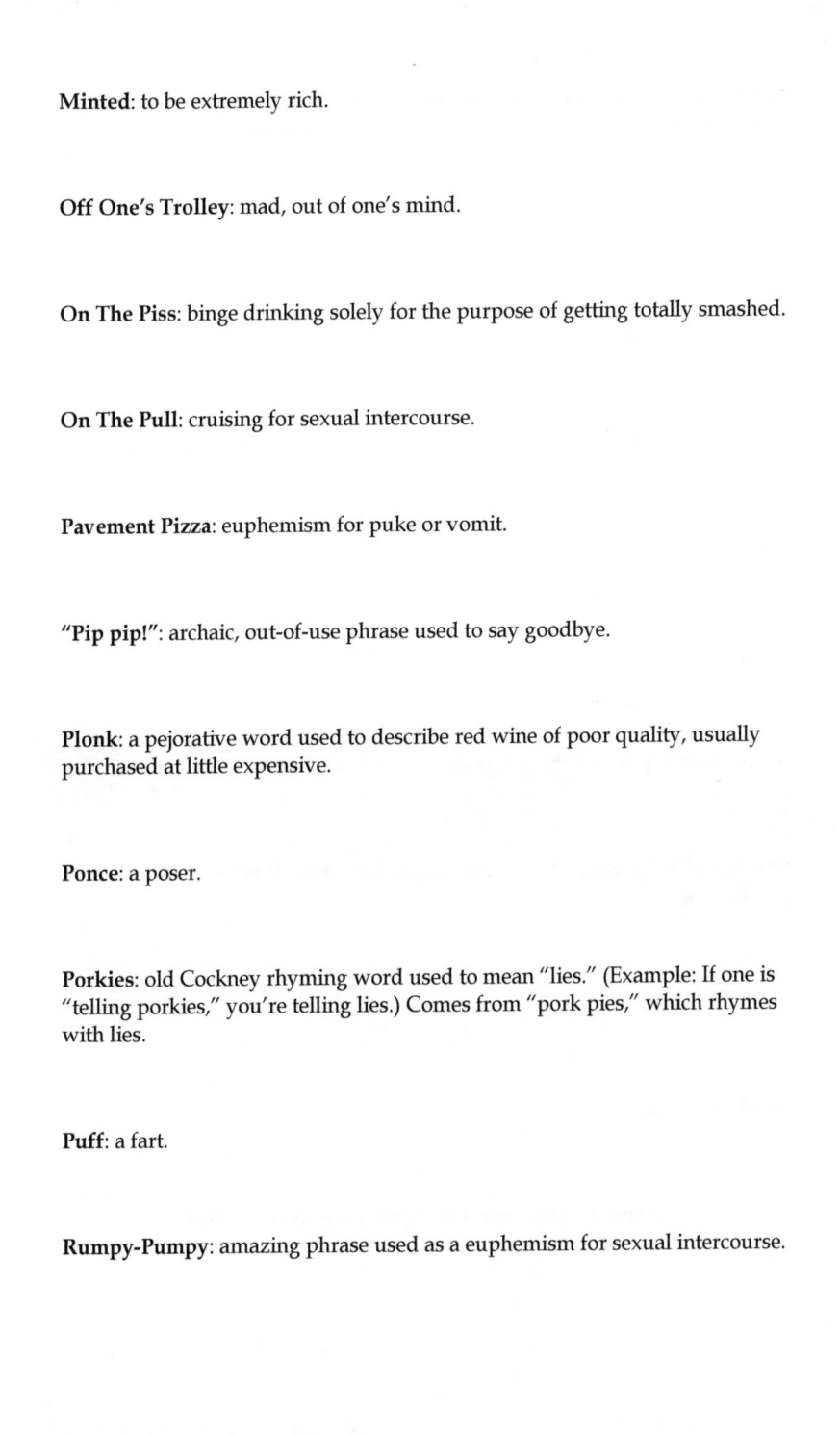

Off One's Trolley: mad, out of one's mind.

On The Piss: binge drinking solely for the purpose of getting totally smashed.

On The Pull: cruising for sexual intercourse.

Pavement Pizza: euphemism for puke or vomit.

"Pip pip!": archaic, out-of-use phrase used to say goodbye.

Plonk: a pejorative word used to describe red wine of poor quality, usually purchased at little expensive.

Ponce: a poser.

Porkies: old Cockney rhyming word used to mean "lies." (Example: If one is "telling porkies," you're telling lies.) Comes from "pork pies," which rhymes with lies.

Puff: a fart.

Rumpy-Pumpy: amazing phrase used as a euphemism for sexual intercourse.

See A Man About a Dog: what you say as an excuse for leaving, in order to hide your destination; also, to excuse oneself to take a giant shit.

Shambolic: in a total state of bedlam, chaos or dismay.

Shirty: ill-tempered, insolent.

Skive: a character deemed particularly lazy or incapable of being of use.

Slap And Tickle: making out or heavy petting.

Slapper: a promiscuous female.

Spend A Penny: to use the restroom.

Snookered: to be in a bad situation, totally fucked or otherwise without a paddle.

Starkers: completely naked.

Stonker: a boner.

Strawberry Creams: hunger-inducing term for a woman's breasts.

Sweet Fanny Adams: code for "Sweet fuck all", meaning little to nothing at all. (Example: "I thought I had a chance with her, but I ended up with Sweet Fanny Adams.)

Taking The Piss: messing or screwing around.

Throw A Spanner In The Works: to make a mistake or fuck up something.

Tickety-Boo: phrase for when everything's going great (Example: "All is tickety-boo in my world.")

Todger: another word for "dick."

Tosh: total bullshit, nonsense or rubbish.

Tosser: derogatory term for male masturbator, used to indicate that you look upon someone unfavorably. (Example: "He fancies himself the bee's knees, but frankly he's quite the wanker.")

Twig And Berries: male genitalia, the penis and balls.

Up The Duff: pregnant or with child.

The Prison Slang

While some words of prison slang are hundreds of years old, others are being introduced all the time. Here are just a few examples:

Pad: a cell. *Come check me in my PAD*
Spin: a search (as in 'pad-spin'). *They SPIN my cell but didn't find my phone.*
Burglars: security or 'DST' ('Dedicated Search Team'). *The DST put me on close viits.*
Bang up: time locked in cell. *Link me before BANG UP ill give you a Tuna.*
Kangas (or 'Scoobys'): screws. *I don't like that SCREW he thinks his hard.*
Midnight: Midnight mass - grass. *Your on some MIDNIGHT ting.*
Ghosting: to be transferred to another prison, suddenly and without notice. *Don't make me send you a V.O (Visiting Order) then you GHOST me.*
Jam-roll: parole. *Hope I get my JAM-ROLL.*
L-Plates: a life sentence. *Everyone on my landing is on a L-PLATE.*
Cucumbers (or 'Numbers' or 'Protection'): 'Nonces' or 'Bacons' (sex offenders) and other 'Protection-heads' (debtors, grasses, cell thieves etc.) are usually segregated for their own safety under Prison Rule 45 (formerly 43). They should not be confused with prisoners held in the block (the segregation unit) under Prison Rule 45 GOAD (Good Order and Discipline).*His a bad man on road but when his in jail his on the numbers lol.*
Stiff: a smuggled note. *Pass this STIFF to my brother on A wing.*
Bed-leg: a homemade cosh. The word comes from the small section of steel pipe used to separate prison bunks, which would be put in a sock to make a weapon. *I hit him with the BED-LEG now I lost my tv.*
Little fellers: cigarette butts. *You got a LITTLE FELLER left bro.*

The enchanted: prisoners on the 'Enhanced Privilege Level'. *Now im ENHANCED I got SKY TV and shower in my cell.*
Tram lines: a distinctive scar caused by a prison-made weapon which uses two razor blades melted into a toothbrush. *My youths got a TRAM LINE WET on his face for life.*
Shit and a shave (or shit and a shower): a short sentence. *Man will be back on road before a SHIT&SHOWER.*
Adidas sex-case: prison issue plimsolls. *Man rocking ADIDAS SEX on his visit.*
Chip-net: safety net strung between landings. *Swing me some food on your CHIP-NET.*
Diesel: prison tea. *She makes a good cup of DIESEL.*

Jimmy or Jimmy Boyle: foil used by smackheads to smoke heroin. *I saw certain road man with the JIMMY smoking B on the landings.*

Wet-up (or Jug-up): to scald someone, usually with a mixture of boiling water and sugar. *He got JUG-UP he hole face came off in his hands.*

Stretch: a sentence or a year (a '10 stretch' is a 10 year sentence).

Peter: an older name for a cell, also for a safe.

Apple or Apple core: Score - 20, hence 20 years or £20. *Lend me A SCORE till pay day im a bit skinned.*

Salmon or Salmon and trout - Snout: tobacco. *Lend me some SNOUT till my canteen come.*

Patches: a prison uniform with prominent yellow panels worn by prisoners captured after an escape or following an attempted escape. *Did you see Jones his in a HEMAN PATCHES.*

Pie and liquor: the vicar. *Ask the PIE & LIQUOR to put a good word in for the open prison application.*

Text Slang, Internet Slang

a$$ - a**
a&f - always and forever
a'ight - alright
a.i.m. - aol instant messanger
a/l - age and location
a/m - away message
a/s/l - age,sex,location
a/s/l/p - age/sex/location/picture
a/s/l/r - age, sex, location, race
a1t - anyone there
a3 - anyplace, anywhere, anytime
aaaaa - American Assosciation Against Acronym Abuse
aabf - as a best friend
aaf - as a friend
aak - Alive and Kicking
aamof - as a matter of fact
aatf - always and totally forever
abd - Already Been Done
abend - absent by enforced net deprivation
abft - About f**king Time
aboot - about
abreev - abbreviation
absnt - absent
abt - about
abwt - about
acc - account
acct - account
acgaf - Absolutely couldn't give a f**k
ack - acknowledged
addy - address
adhd - Attention Deficit Hyperactivity Disorder
adl - all day long
admin - administrator
adn - any day now
aeap - as early as possible

af - assface
afaiaa - As Far As I Am Aware
afaic - As far as I'm concerned
afaicr - As Far As I Can Remember
afaics - As far as I can see
afaict - As far as I can tell
afaik - As far as I know
afair - As far as I recall
afaiu - As far as I understand
afc - Away from computer
afcpmgo - Away from computer parents may go on
afg - away from game
afk - away from keyboard
afkb - away from keyboard
agn - again
ah - a** hole
ahole - a**h**e
ai - Artificial Intelligence
aiadw - ALL IN A DAYS WORK
aiamu - and I'm a monkey's uncle
aicmfp - and I claim my five pounds
aight - Alright
aightz - alright
aiic - as if I care
aiid - and if I did
aiight - all right
aim - AOL instant messanger
ain't - am not
aite - Alright
aitr - Adult in the room
aiui - as I understand it
aiws - as i was saying
ajax - Asynchronous Javascript and XML
aka - also known as
akp - Alexander King Project
akpcep - Alexander King Project Cultural Engineering Project
alaytm - as long as you tell me
alol - actually laughing out loud
alot - a lot
alotbsol - always look on the bright side of life

alright - all right
alrite - Alright
alrt - alright
alryt - alright
ama - ask me anything
amf - adios motherf**ker
amiic - ask me if i care
amiigaf - ask me if i give a f**k
aml - All My Love
amsp - ask me something personal
anim8 - animate
anl - all night long
anlsx - Anal Sex
anon - anonymous
anuda - another
anw - anyways
anwwi - alright now where was i
any1 - Anyone
anywaz - anyways
aob - any other business
aoc - age of consent
aoe - Age Of Empires
aon - all or nothing
aos - adult over shoulder
aota - all of the above
aoto - Amen on that one
aoys - angel on your shoulder
api - application program interface
apoc - apocalypse
apod - Another Point Of Discussion
app - application
appt - appointment
aprece8 - appreciate
apreci8 - appreciate
apu - as per usual
aqap - as quick as possible
ar - are
arnd - around
arse - a**
arsed - bothered

arvo - afternoon
asafp - as soon as f**king possible
asaik - as soon as I know
asap - as soon as possible
asarbambtaa - All submissions are reviewed by a moderator before they are added.
asbmaetp - Acronyms should be memorable and easy to pronounce
ase - age, sex, ethnicity
ashl - a**h**e
ashole - a**h**e
asic - application specific integrated circuit
asl - age, sex, location
aslo - age sex location orientation
aslop - Age Sex Location Orientation Picture
aslp - age, sex, location, picture
aslr - age sex location race
aslrp - age, sex, location, race, picture
asr - age sex race
asshle - a**h**e
atb - all the best
atfp - answer the f**king phone
atl - atlanta
atm - at the moment
ato - against the odds
atop - at time of posting
atp - answer the phone
atq - answer the question
atst - At the same time
attn - attention
attotp - At The Time Of This Post
atw - All the way
aty - according to you
audy - Are you done yet?
aufm - are you f**king mental
aufsm - are you f**king shiting me
aup - acceptable use policy
av7x - avenged sevenfold
avgn - Angry Video Game Nerd
avie - Avatar

avsb - a very special boy
avtr - avatar
avvie - avatar
avy - Avatar
awes - awesome
awk - awkward
awol - absent without leave
awsic - and why should i care
awsm - awesome
awsome - awesome
ayagob - are you a girl or boy
ayb - All Your Base
aybab2m - all your base are belong 2 me
aybab2u - All your base are belong to us
aybabtg - All Your Base Are Belong To Google
aybabtu - all your base are belong to us
ayc - awaiting your comments
ayd - are you done
aydy - are you done yet
ayec - at your earliest convenience
ayfk - are you f**king kidding
ayfkm - are you f**king kidding me
ayfr - are you for real
ayfs - Are You f**king Serious
ayk - are you kidding
aykm - are you kidding me
ayl - are you listening
aymf - are you my friend
ayok - are you okay
aypi - And Your Point Is
aypi - and your point is
ays - are you serious
aysm - are you shitting me?
ayst - are you still there
ayt - are you there
ayte - alright
aytf - are you there f**ker
ayty - are you there yet
ayw - as you wish
azhol - a**h**e

azn - asian
azz - a**
bi - bye
b& - banned
b'day - birthday
b-cuz - because
b-day - birthday
b.f.f. - best friend forever
b.s. - bulls**t
b/c - because
b/cos - because
b/g - background
b/s/l - Bisexual/Straight/Lesbian
b/t - between
b/w - between
b00n - new person
b00t - boot
b0rked - broken
b1tch - b***h
b2b - business to business
b2u - back to you
b2w - Back to work
b3 - be
b4 - before
b4n - bye for now
b4u - before you
b8 - bait
b82rez - Batteries
b8rez - Batteries
b@ - banned
bab - Big a** Boobs
babi - baby
baf - bring a friend
baggkyko - be a good girl, keep your knickers on
bah - I don't really care
bai - Bye
bak - back
bakk - back
balz - balls
bamf - bad a** mother f**ker

bamofo - b***h a** mother f**ker
bau - back at you
bb - bye bye
bb4h - bros before hoes
bb4n - bye-bye for now
bbbj - bare Back Blow Job
bbe - baby
bbf - best boy friend
bbfn - bye Bye for now
bbfs - best boyfriends
bbfu - be back for you
bbi - Baby
bbiab - be back in a bit
bbiaf - be back in a few
bbialb - be back in a little bit
bbiam - be back in a minute
bbias - be back in a second
bbiaw - be back in a while
bbifs - be back in a few seconds
bbilb - be back in a little bit
bbilfm - be back in like five minutes
bbim - be back In Minute
bbk - be back, ok?
bbl - be back later
bbl8a - be Back Later
bblig - be back later...i guess
bbm - blackBerry Messenger
bbml - be back much later
bbn - be back never
bbol - be back online later
bbp - banned by parents
bbq - be back quick
bbrs - be back really soon
bbs - be back soon
bbsts - be back some time soon
bbt - be back tomorrow
bbtn - be back tonite
bbvl - be Back Very Later
bbw - be back whenever
bbwb - best buddy with boobs

bbwe - be back whenever
bbwl - be back way later
bby - baby
bbz - babes
bc - because
bch - b***h
bck - back
bcnu - be seeing you
bcnul8r - be seeing you later
bcoz - because
bcurl8 - because you're late.
bcuz - because
bd - birthday
bday - birthday
bdfl - benevolent Dictator For Life
be4 - before
beatch - b***h
bebe - baby
becuse - because
becuz - because
beech - b***h
beeoch - b***h
beezy - b***h
beotch - b***h
besos - kisses
bestie - best friend
betch - b***h
betcha - bet you
bettr - better
bewb - boob
bewbs - boobs
bewbz - boobs
bewt - boot
beyatch - b***h
beyotch - b***h
bezzie - best friend
bf - boyfriend
bf's - boyfriend's
bf+gf - boyfriend and girlfriend
bf4e - best friends for ever

bf4eva - Best Friends forever
bf4l - best friends for life
bfam - brother from another mother
bfd - big f**king deal
bfe - Bum f**k Egypt
bff - best friend forever
bffa - best friends for always
bffaa - Best Friends Forever And Always
bffae - Best Friends Forever And Ever
bffaw - best friends for a while
bffe - Best friends forever
bffeae - Best Friend For Ever And Ever
bffene - Best Friends For Ever And Ever
bffl - best friends for life
bffn - best friends for now
bfftddup - best friends forever till death do us part
bfg - big f**king gun
bfh - b***h from hell
bfhd - big fat hairy deal
bfitww - best friend in the whole world
bfn - bye for now
bfs - Boyfriends
bft - big f**king tits
bg - background
bh - bloody hell
bhwu - back home with you
biab - back in a bit
biach - b***h
biaf - Back In A Few
biatch - b***h
bibi - bye bye
bibifn - bye bye for now
bicbw - but I could be wrong
bich - b***h
bigd - big deal
bii - bye
bilf - brother i'd like to f**k
bilu - baby i love you
bion - Believe it or not.
biotch - b***h

bioya - blow it out your a**
bish - b***h
bitd - back in the day
biw - boss is watching
biwm - bisexual white male
biz - Business
bizatch - b***h
bizi - Busy
biznatch - b***h
biznitch - b***h
bizzle - b***h
bj - blowjob
bk - back
bka - better known as
bl - bad luck
bleme - blog meme
bleve - believe
blg - blog
blh - bored like hell
bling-bling - jewelry
blj - blowjob
bljb - Blowjob
blk - black
blkm - Black Male
blnt - Better Luck Next time
blog - web log
blogger - web logger
blu - blue
bm - Bite Me
bm&y - between you and me
bm4l - best mates for life
bma - best mates always
bmay - between me and you
bmf - be my friend
bmfe - best mates forever
bmfl - best mates for life
bmha - bite my hairy a**
bml - bless my life
bmoc - Big Man On Campus
bmttveot - best mates till the very end of time

bmvp - be my valentine please
bn - been
bndm3ovr - Bend me over
bng - being
bnib - Brand new in Box
bnol - be nice or leave
bnr - banner
bo - body odour
boati - Bend Over And Take It
bobfoc - Body of Baywatch, Face of Crimewatch
bobw - Best of Both Worlds
boffum - Both of them
bofh - b*****d operator from hell
bogo - buy one get one
bogof - buy one get one free
bogsatt - bunch of guys sitting around the table
bohic - Bend over here it comes
bohica - bend over, here it comes again
boi - boy
bol - Barking Out Loud
bonr - boner
boomm - bored out of my mind
bord - bored
bos - boss over shoulder
botoh - but on the other hand
bout - about
bovered - bothered
bowt - about
boxor - box
bpot - big pair of tits
br - bathroom
brb - be right back
brbbrb - br right back bath room break
brbf - Be Right Back f**ker
brbg2p - be right back, got to pee
brbigtp - be right back, i got to pee.
brbl - be right back later
brbmf - be right back mother f**ker
brbn2gbr - Be right back, I need to go to the bathroom
brbs - be right back soon

brbts - be right back taking s**t
brd - bored
brfb - be right f**king back
brgds - best regards
brh - be right here
bro - brother
bros - brothers
broseph - brother
brover - Brother
brt - be right there
bruh - brother
bruhh - Brother
bruv - brother
bruva - brother
bruz - brothers
bs - bulls**t
bsmfh - b*****d System Manager From Hell
bsod - blue screen of death
bsomn - blowing stuff out my nose
bstfu - b***h shut the f**k up
bstrd - b*****d
bsx - bisexual
bsxc - be sexy
bt - bit torrent
btb - by the by
btch - b***h
btcn - Better than Chuck Norris
btd - bored to death
btdt - been there done that
btdtgtts - Been there, done that, got the T-shirt
btfl - beautiful
btfo - back the f**k off
btfw - by the f**king way
btias - Be there in a second
btm - bottom
btr - better
bts - be there soon
btsoom - Beats The s**t Out Of Me
bttt - been there, tried that
bttyl - be talking to you later

btw - by the way
btwilu - by the way i love you
btwitiailwu - by the way i think i am in love with you
btwn - between
bty - back to you
bubar - bushed up beyond all recognition
bubi - bye
budzecks - butt sex
buhbi - Bye Bye
bukket - bucket
bur - p***y
burma - be undressed ready my angel
buszay - busy
but6 - buttsex
butsecks - butt sex
butterface - every thing is hot but her face
buwu - breaking up with you
bw3 - Buffalo Wild Wings
bwim - by which i mean
bwoc - Big Woman On Campus
bwpwap - back when Pluto was a planet
bwt - but when though
byak - blowing you a kiss
byeas - good-bye
byes - bye bye
bykt - But you knew that
byob - Bring your own Beer
byoc - bring our own computer
byself - by myself
bytabm - beat you to a bloody mess
bytch - b***h
bz - busy
bzns - buisness
bzy - busy
bzzy - busy
c - see
c 2 c - cam to cam (webcams)
c&c - Command and Conquer
c'mon - Come On
c-p - sleepy

c.y.a - cover your a**
c/b - comment back
c/t - can't talk
c14n - canonicalization
c2 - come to
c2c - care to chat?
c2tc - cut to the chase
c4ashg - care for a shag
c@ - cat
cam - camera
cancer stick - cigarette
catwot - complete and total waste of time
cawk - c**k
cayc - call at your convenience
cb - come back
cba - can't be arsed
cbb - can't be bothered
cbf - cant be f**ked
cbfa - can't be f**king arsed
cbfed - can't be f**ked
cbi - can't believe it
ccl - Couldn't Care Less
ccna - Cisco Certified Network Associate
cd9 - Code 9 (other people nearby)
celly - cell phone
cex - sex
cexy - sexy
cfas - care for a secret?
cfid - check for identification
cfm - come f**k me
cg - Congratulations
cgad - couldn't give a d**n
cgaf - couldn't give a f**k
cgf - cute guy friend
ch@ - chat
champs - champions
char - character
cheezburger - cheeseburger
chik - chick
chilax - chill and relax in one word

chillax - chill and relax
chillin - relaxing
chk - check
chohw - Come Hell or high water
chr - character
chronic - marijuana
chswm - come have sex with me
chswmrn - come have sex with me right now
chu - you
chut - p***y
cid - consider it done
cig - cigarette
cigs - cigarettes
cihswu - can i have sex with you
cihyn - can i have your number
cilf - child i'd like to f**k
cing - seeing
cis - computer information science
ciwwaf - cute is what we aim for
cless - clanless
clm - Cool Like Me
clt - Cool Like That
cluebie - clueless newbie
cm - call me
cma - Cover My a**
cmao - Crying My a** Off
cmar - cry me a river
cmb - comment me back
cmbo - combo
cmcp - call my cell phone
cmeo - crying my eyes out
cmh - Call My House
cmiiw - correct me if I'm wrong
cmitm - Call me in the morning
cml - call me later
cml8r - call me later
cmliuw2 - call me later if you want to
cmomc - call me on my cell
cmon - Come on
cmplcdd - complicated

cmplte - complete
cmptr - computer
cms - content management system
cmt - comment
cmw - cutting my wrists
cn - can
cnc - Command and Conquer
cnt - can't
cob - close of business
cod - Call of Duty
cod4 - call of duty 4
cod5 - call of duty 5
code 29 - moderator is watching
code 8 - parents are watching
code 9 - Parents are watching
code9 - other people near by
cof - Crying on the floor
coiwta - come on i wont tell anyone
col - crying out loud
comin' - coming
comnt - comment
comp - Computer
compy - computer
congrats - congratulations
contrib - contribution
contribs - contributions
convo - conversation
coo - cool
cood - could
copyvio - copyright violation
cos - because
cotf - crying on the floor
cotm - check out this myspace
cowboy choker - cigarette
coz - because
cp - child porn
cpl - Cyber Athlete Professional League
cpm - cost per 1000 impressions
cptn - captain
cpy - copy

cr - Can't remember
cr8 - **crate**
crakalakin - happening
crazn - crazy asian
cre8or - creator
crm - customer relationship management
crp - crap
crs - can't remember s**t
crunk - combination of crazy and drunk
crzy - crazy
cs - Counter-Strike
cs:s - Counter-Strike: Source
csi - Crime Scene Investigation
cskr - c**k sucker
csl - can't stop laughing
ct - can't talk
ctc - call the cell
ctf - capture the flag
ctfd - calm the f**k down
ctfo - chill the f**k out
ctfu - cracking the f**k up
ctm - chuckle to myself
ctn - can't talk now
ctnbos - can't talk now boss over shoulder
ctncl - Can't talk now call later
ctpc - cant talk parent(s) coming
ctpos - Can't Talk Parent Over Sholder
ctrl - control
ctrn - can't talk right now
cts - change the subject
ctt - change the topic
cu - goodbye
cu2nit - see you tonight
cu46 - see you for sex
cubi - can you believe it
cud - could
cuic - see you in cla**
cul - see you later
cul83r - See you later
cul8er - see you later

cul8r - See You Later
cul8tr - see you later
culd - Could
cunt - vagina
cuom - see you on monday
cuple - couple
curn - calling you right now
cut3 - cute
cuwul - catch up with you later
cuz - because
cuzz - Because
cvq - chucking very quietly
cw2cu - can`t wait to see you
cwm - come with me
cwmaos - coffee with milk and one sugar
cwot - complete waste of time
cwtgypo - can't wait to get your panties off
cwyl - chat with ya later
cya - goodbye
cyal - see you later
cyal8r - see you later
cyas - see you soon
cyb - cyber
cybl - call you back later
cybr - cyber
cybseckz - cyber sex
cye - Close Your Eyes
cyff - change your font, f**ker
cyl - see you later
cyl,a - see ya later, alligator
cyl8 - see you later
cyl8er - see you later
cylbd - catch ya later baby doll
cylor - check your local orhtodox rabbi
cym - check your mail
cyntott - see you next time on Tech Today
cyt - see you tomorrow
cyu - see you
c|n>k - coffee through nose into keyboard
d&c - divide and conquer

d&df - drug & disease free
d.t.f - down to f**k
d.w - don't worry
d/c - disconnected
d/l - download
d/m - Doesn't Matter
d/w - don't worry
d00d - dude
d1ck - d**k
d2 - Diablo 2
d2m - dead to me
d2t - drink to that
d8 - date
da - the
da2 - Dragon Age 2
dadt - Don't ask. Don't tell.
dafs - do a f**king search
dah - dumb as hell
daii - day
damhik - don't ask me how I know
damhikijk - Don't Ask Me How I Know - I Just Know
damhikt - don't ask me how I know this
dass - dumb a**
dat - that
dats - that's
dawg - Friend
dayum - d**n
dayumm - d**n
db - database
db4l - drinking buddy for life
dbab - don't be a b***h
dbafwtt - Don't Be A Fool Wrap The Tool
dbag - d****ebag
dbeyr - don't believe everything you read
dbg - don't be gay
dbh - don't be hating
dbi - Don't Beg It
dbm - don't bother me
dbz - DragonBall Z
dc - don't care

dc'd - disconnected
dctnry - dictionary
dcw - Doing Cla** Work
dd - don't die
ddf - Drug and Disease Free
ddg - Drop Dead Gorgeous
ddl - direct download
ddos - Distributed Denial of Service
ddr - dance dance revolution
deets - details
deez - these
def - definitely
defs - definetly
degmt - Don't Even Give Me That
dem - them
der - there
dernoe - I don't know
detai - don't even think about it
dewd - Dude
dey - they
df - Dumb f**k
dfc - DON'T f**kING CARE
dfo - dumb f**king operator
dftba - don't forget to be awesome
dftc - down for the count
dfu - don't f**k up
dfw - down for whatever
dfw/m - Don't f**k with Me
dfwm - Don't f**k with Me
dfwmt - Don't f**king waste my time
dg - don't go
dga - don't go anywhere
dgac - don't give a crap
dgaf - don't give a f**k
dgara - don't give a rats a**
dgas - Don't give a s**t
dgms - Don't get me started
dgoai - don't go on about it
dgt - don't go there
dgypiab - don't get your panties in a bunch

dh - dickhead
dhac - Don't have a clue
dhly - does he like you
dhv - Demonstration of Higher Value
diacf - die in a car fire
diaf - die in a fire
diah - die in a hole
dic - do i care
dick - penis
diez - dies
diff - difference
dih - d**k in hand
dikhed - dickhead
diku - do i know you
diky - Do I know you
dil - Daughter in law
dilf - dad i'd like to f**k
dillic - Do I look like I care
dillifc - do I look like I f**king care
dilligad - do I look like I give a d**n
dilligaf - do I look like I give a f**k
dilligas - do i look like i give a s**t
din - didn't
din't - didn't
dirl - Die in real life
dis - this
dit - Details in Thread
diy - do it yourself
dju - did you
dk - don't know
dkdc - don't know, don't care
dl - download
dlf - dropping like flies
dlibu - Dont let it bother you
dln - don't look now
dm - deathmatch
dmaf - do me a favor
dmba* - dumba**
dmi - don't mention it
dmn - d**n

dmu - don't mess up
dmwm - don't mess with me
dmy - don't mess yourself
dn - don't know
dnd - Do Not Disturb
dndp - Do not double post
dnimb - dancing naked in my bra
dno - don't know
dnrta - did not read the article
dnrtfa - did not read the f**king article
dns - Domain Name System
dnt - don't
dnw - Do not want
doa - dead on arrival
dob - date of birth
dod - Day of Defeat
dogg - friend
doin - doing
doin' - doing
don - denial of normal
doncha - Don't you
donno - don't know
dont - don't
dontcha - don't you
dood - dude
doodz - dudes
dos - denial of service
dotc - dancing on the ceiling
doypov - depends on your point of view
dp - display picture
dpmo - don't piss me off
dprsd - depressed
dqmot - don't quote me on this
dqydj - don't quit your day job
dr00d - druid
drc - don't really care
drm - dream
drood - druid
dsided - decided
dsu - don't screw up

dt - double team
dta - Don't Trust Anyone
dtb - don't text back
dth - down to hang
dtl - d**n the luck
dtp - Don't Type Please
dtrt - do the right thing
dts - Don't think so
dttm - don't talk to me
dttml - don't talk to me loser
dttpou - Don't tell the police on us
dttriaa - don't tell the RIAA
du2h - d**n you to hell
ducy - do you see why
dugi - do you get it?
dugt - did you get that?
duk - did you know
dulm - do you like me
dum - dumb
dun - don't
dunna - i don't know
dunno - I don't know
duno - don't know
dupe - duplicate
dutma - don't you text me again
dvda - double vaginal, double anal
dw - don't worry
dwai - don't worry about it
dwb - Driving while black
dwbh - don't worry, be happy
dwbi - Don't worry about it.
dwi - deal with it
dwioyot - Deal With It On Your Own Time
dwmt - don't waste my time
dwn - down
dwt - don't wanna talk
dwy - don't wet yourself
dy2h - d**n you to hell
dya - Do you
dyac - d**n you auto correct

dycotfc - do you cyber on the first chat
dyec - Don't You Ever Care
dygtp - did you get the picture
dyk - did you know
dylh - do you like him
dylm - do you love me
dylos - do you like oral sex
dym - Do you mind
dynk - do you not know
dynm - do you know me
dyt - Don't you think
dyth - d**n You To Hell
dyw - don't you worry
dyw2gwm - do you want to go with me
dywtmusw - do you want to meet up some where
e-ok - Electronically OK
e.g. - example
e4u2s - easy for you to say
eabod - eat a bag of dicks
ead - eat a d**k
ebitda - earnings before interest, taxes, depreciation and amortization
ecf - error carried forward
edumacation - education
eedyat - idiot
eejit - idiot
ef - f**k
ef-ing - f**king
efct - effect
efffl - extra friendly friends for life
effin - f**king
effing - f**king
eg - evil grin
ehlp - help
eil - explode into laughter
el!t - elite
eleo - Extremely Low Earth Orbit
ello - hello
elo - hello
em - them

emm - email me
emo - emotional
emp - eat my p***y
enat - every now and then
enit - isn't it
enof - enough
enuf - enough
enuff - enough
eob - End of Business
eoc - end of conversation
eod - End of day
eof - end of file
eom - end of message
eos - end of story
eot - end of transmission
eotw - end of the world
epa - Emergency Parent Alert
eq - Everquest
eq2 - Everquest2
ere - here
errythin - everything
esad - eat s**t and die
esadyffb - eat s**t and die you fat f**king b*****d
esbm - Everyone sucks but me
esc - escape
esl - eat s**t loser
eta - Estimated Time of Arrival
etla - extended three letter acronym
etmda - Explain it to my dumb a**
etp - eager to please
eula - end user license agreement
ev1 - everyone
eva - ever
evaa - ever
evar - ever
evercrack - Everquest
every1 - everyone
evn - even
evr - ever
evry - every

evry1 - every one
evrytin - everything
ex-bf - Ex-Boy Friend
ex-gf - Ex-Girl Friend
exp - experience
ey - hey
eyez - eyes
ez - Easy
ezi - easy
f u - f**k you
f#cking - f**king
f&e - forever and ever
f'n - f**king
f-ing - f**king
f.b. - facebook
f.m.l. - f**k my life
f.u. - f**k you
f/o - f**k off
f00k - f**k.
f2f - face to face
f2p - free to play
f2t - Free to talk
f4c3 - face
f4eaa - friends forever and always
f4f - female for female
f4m - female for male
f8 - fate
f9 - fine
f@ - fat
fa-q - f**k you
faa - forever and always
fab - fabulous
faggit - faggot
fah - Funny as hell
faic - For All I Care
fam - family
fankle - area between foot and ankle
fao - for attention of
fap - masturbate
fapping - masterbating

faq - frequently asked question
farg - f**k
fashizzle - for sure
fav - Favorite
fave - favorite
fawk - f**k
fbimcl - Fall Back In My Chair Laughing
fbk - facebook
fbtw - Fine Be That Way
fc - fruit cake
fcbk - facebook
fcfs - first come first served
fck - f**k
fckd - f**ked
fckin - f**king
fcking - f**king
fckm3hdbayb - f**k Me Hard Baby
fcku - f**k you
fcol - for crying out loud
fcuk - f**k
fe - fatal error
feck - f**k
fer - for
ferr - For
ff - friendly fire
ffa - free for all
ffcl - falling from chair laughing
ffr - for future reference
ffs - for f**k's sake
fft - food for thought
ffxi - Final Fantasy 11
fg - f**king gay
fgi - f**king google it
fgs - for God's sake
fgssu - For Gods sake shut up
fgt - faggot
fi - f**k it
fi9 - fine
fibijar - f**k it buddy, I'm just a reserve
fifo - first in, first out

fify - Fixed It For You
figjam - f**k I'm good, just ask me
figmo - F*ck it - got my orders
fiic - f**ked If I Care
fiik - f**ked If I Know
fimh - forever in my heart
fio - figure it out
fitb - fill in the blank
fiv - five
fk - f**k
fka - formerly known as
fker - f**ker
fkin - f**king
fking - f**king
fkn - f**king
fku - f**k you
flamer - angry poster
flames - angry comments
flicks - pictures
floabt - for lack of a better term
fm - f**k me
fmah - f**k my a** hole
fmao - freezing my a** of
fmb - f**k me b***h
fmbb - f**k Me Baby
fmbo - f**k my brains out
fmfl - f**k my f**king life
fmflth - f**k My f**king Life To Hell
fmh - f**k me hard
fmhb - f**k me hard b***h
fmi - for my information
fmir - family member in room
fmita - f**k me in the a**
fml - f**k my life
fmltwia - f**k me like the w***e I am
fmn - f**k me now
fmnb - f**k me now b***h
fmnkml - f**k me now kiss me later
fmph - f**k my p***y hard
fmq - f**k me quick

fmr - f**k me runnig
fmsh - f**k me so hard
fmth - f**k me to hell
fmuta - f**k me up the a**
fmutp - f**k me up the p***y
fn - first name
fnar - For No Apparent Reason
fnci - fancy
fnny - funny
fnpr - for no particular reason
fny - funny
fo - f**k off
fo shizzle - for sure
fo sho - for sure
foa - f**k off a**h**e
foad - f**k off and die
foaf - friend of a friend
foah - f**k off a**h**e
fob - fresh off the boat
focl - Falling Off Chair Laughing.
fofl - fall on the floor laughing
foia - freedom of information act
fol - farting out loud
folo - Follow
fomofo - f**k off mother f**ker
fone - phone
foo - fool
foobar - f**ked up beyond all recognition
foocl - falls out of chair laughing
fook - f**k
for sheeze - for sure
fos - full of s**t
foshizzle - for sure
fosho - for sure
foss - free, open source software
fotcl - fell off the chair laughing
fotm - Flavour of the month
fouc - f**k off you c**t
fov - Field of View
foyb - f**k off you b***h

fo` - for
fp - first post
fpmitap - federal pound me in the a** prison
fpos - f**king piece of s**t
fps - First Person Shooter
frag - kill
fragged - killed
fren - friend
frens - friends
frgt - forgot
fri. - Friday
friggin - freaking
frk - freak
frm - from
frnd - friend
frnds - friends
fs - For Sure
fsho - for sure
fsm - flying spaghetti monster
fsob - f**king son of a b***h
fsod - frosn screen of death
fsr - for some reason
fst - fast
ft - f**k THAT
ft2t - From time to time
fta - From The Article
ftb - f**k That b***h
ftbfs - Failed to build from source
ftf - face to face
ftfa - From The f**king Article
ftfw - For the f**king win!
ftfy - Fixed that for you
ftio - fun time is over
ftk - For the Kill
ftl - For The Lose
ftlog - for the love of god
ftlt - For the last time
ftmfw - for the mother f**king win
ftmp - For the most part
ftp - file transfer protocol

ftr - For The Record
fts - f**k that s**t
fttp - for the time being
ftw - For the win!
fu - f**k you
fua - f**k you all
fuah - f**k you a** hole
fub - f**k you b***h
fubah - f**ked up beyond all hope
fubalm - f**ked up beyond all local maintenance
fubar - f**ked up beyond all recognition
fubb - f**ked up beyond belief
fubh - f**ked up beyond hope
fubohic - f**k you Bend over here it comes
fubr - f**ked Up Beyond Recognition
fucken - f**king
fucktard - f**king retard
fuctard - f**king retard
fud - fear, uncertainty and doubt
fudh - f**k you d**k head
fudie - f**k you and die
fugly - f**king ugly
fuh-q - f**k you
fuhget - forget
fuk - f**k
fukin - f**king
fukk - f**k
fukkin - f**king
fukn - f**king
fukr - f**ker
fulla - Full of
fumfer - f**k you mother f**ker
funee - funny
funner - more fun
funy - funny
fuq - f**k you
fus - f**k yourself
fut - f**k You Too
fuu - f**k you up
fux - f**k

fuxing - f**king
fuxor - f**ker
fuxored - f**ked
fvck - f**k
fwb - Friends with Benefits
fwd - forward
fwiw - for what it's worth
fwm - Fine With Me
fwob - friends with occasional benefits
fxe - foxy
fxp - file exchange protocol
fy - f**k you
fya - for your attention
fyad - f**k you and die
fyah - f**k you a**h**e
fyb - f**k you b***h
fyc - f**k your couch
fye - For Your Entertainment
fyeo - For your eyes only
fyf - f**k your face
fyfi - For Your f**king Information
fyi - for your information
fyk - for your knowledge
fyl - For your Love
fym - f**k your mom
fyp - fixed your post
fyrb - f**k you right back
g - grin
g'nite - good night
g/f - girlfriend
g/g - got to go
g0 - go
g00g13 - Google
g1 - good one
g2 - go to
g2/-/ - go to hell
g2bg - got to be going
g2bl8 - going to be late
g2cu - glad to see you
g2e - got to eat

g2g - got to go
g2g2tb - got to go to the bathroom
g2g2w - got to go to work
g2g4aw - got to go for a while
g2gb - got to go bye
g2gb2wn - got to go back to work now
g2ge - got to go eat
g2gn - got to go now
g2gp - got to go pee
g2gpc - got 2 go parents coming
g2gpp - got to go pee pee
g2gs - got to go sorry
g2h - go to hell
g2hb - go to hell b***h
g2k - good to know
g2p - got to pee
g2t2s - got to talk to someone
g3y - gay
g4u - good for you
g4y - good for you
g8 - gate
g9 - good night
g@y - gay
ga - go ahead
gaalma - go away and leave me alone
gaf - good as f**k
gafi - get away from it
gafl - get a f**king life
gafm - Get away from me
gagf - go and get f**ked
gagp - go and get pissed
gah - gay a** homo
gai - gay
gaj - get a job
gal - get a life
gamez - illegally obtained games
gangsta - gangster
gank - kill
gaoep - generally accepted office etiquette principles
gaw - grandparents are watching

gawd - god
gb - Go back
gb2 - go back to
gba - game boy advance
gbioua - Go blow it out your a**
gbnf - Gone but not forgotten
gbtw - go back to work
gbu - god bless you
gby - good bye
gcad - get cancer and die
gcf - Google Click Fraud
gd - good
gd&r - grins, ducks, and runs
gd4u - Good For You
gday - Good Day
gdby - good bye
gded - grounded
gdgd - good good
gdi - God d**n it
gdiaf - go die in a fire
gdih - Go die in hell
gdilf - Grandad I'd Like To f**k
gdmfpos - god d**n mother f**king piece of s**t
gdr - grinning, ducking, running
gemo - gay emo
getcha - get you
geto - ghetto
gewd - good
gey - gay
gf - girlfriend
gfad - go f**k a duck
gfadh - go f**k a dead horse
gfak - go fly a kite
gfam - Go f**k A Monkey
gfar2cu - go find a rock to crawl under
gfas - go f**k a sheep
gfd - god f**king damnit
gfe - Girl Friend experience
gfe2e - grinning from ear to ear
gfg - good f**king game

gfgi - go f**king google it
gfi - good f**king idea
gfj - good f**king job
gfl - grounded for life
gfo - go f**k off
gfu - go f**k yourself
gfurs - go f**k yourself
gfus - go f**k yourself
gfx - graphics
gfy - good for you
gfyd - go f**k your dad
gfym - go f**k your mom
gfys - go f**k yourself
gg - good game
gga - good game all
ggal - go get a life
ggf - go get f**ked
ggg - Go, go, go!
ggnore - good game no rematch
ggp - gotta go pee
ggpaw - gotta go parents are watching
ggs - good games
gh - good half
ghei - Gay
ghey - gay
gigig - get it got it good
gigo - garbage in garbage out
gilf - Grandma I'd like to f**k
gim - google instant messanger
gimme - give me
gimmie - give me
gir - google it retard
gis - Google Image Search
gitar - guitar
giv - give
giyf - google is your friend
gj - good job
gjial - go jump in a lake
gjp - good job partner
gjsu - god just shut up

gjt - good job team
gky - Go kill yourself
gkys - Go kill yourself
gl - good luck
gl hf - good luck, have fun
gl&hf - good luck and have fun
gla - good luck all
glbt - Gay, lesbian, bisexual, transgenderd
glf - group looking for
glhf - good luck have fun
glln - Got Laid Last Night
glnhf - Good Luck and Have Fun
glty - Good luck this year
glu - girl like us
glu2 - good luck to you too
glux - good luck
glwt - good luck with that
gm - good morning
gma - grandma
gmab - give me a break
gmabj - give me a blowjob
gmafb - give me a f**king break
gmao - Giggling my a** off
gmfao - Giggling My f**king a** Off
gmilf - grandmother i'd like to f**k
gmod - Global Moderator
gmta - great minds think alike
gmtyt - good morning to you too
gmv - Got my vote
gmybs - give me your best shot
gn - good night
gn8 - good night
gnasd - good night and sweet dreams
gndn - Goes nowhere,does nothing
gnfpwlbn - good news for people who love bad news
gng - going
gng2 - going to
gngbng - gang bang
gnight - good night
gnite - good night

gnn - get naked now
gno - going to do
gnoc - get naked on cam
gnos - get naked on screen
gnr - Guns n' roses
gnrn - get naked right now
gnst - goodnight sleep tight
gnstdltbbb - good night sleep tight don't let the bed bugs bite
goc - get on camera
goi - get over it
goia - get over it already
goin - going
gok - God Only Knows
gokid - got observers - keep it decent
gokw - God Only Knows Why
gol - giggle out loud
gomb - get off my back
goml - get out of my life
gona - Gonna
gonna - going to
good9 - goodnite
gooh - get out of here!
goomh - get out of my head
gork - God only really knows
gosad - go suck a d**k
gotc - get on the computer
gotcha - got you
gotta - got to
gow - gears of war
goya - Get Off Your a**
goyhh - get off your high horse
gp - good point
gpb - gotta pee bad
gpwm - good point well made
gpytfaht - gladly pay you tuesday for a hamburger today
gr8 - great
gr8t - great
grats - congratulations
gratz - congratulations
grfx - graphics

grillz - metal teeth
grl - girl
grmbl - grumble
grog - beer
grrl - Girl
grtg - Getting ready to go
grvy - groovy
gsad - go suck a d**k
gsave - global struggle against violent extremists
gsd - getting s**t done
gsfg - Go search f**king google
gsi - go suck it
gsoh - Good Sense of Humor
gsp - get some p***y
gsta - Gangster
gt - get
gta - Grand Theft Auto
gtas - go take a s**t
gtb - Go To Bed
gtf - get the f**k
gtfa - Go The f**k Away
gtfbtw - get the f**k back to work
gtfh - go to f**king hell
gtfo - get the f**k out
gtfoi - get the f**k over it
gtfon - Get the f**k out noob
gtfooh - get the f**k out of here
gtfoomf - get the f**k out of my face
gtfu - grow the f**k up
gtfuotb - get the f**k up out this b***h
gtg - got to go
gtgbb - got to go bye bye
gtgfn - got to go for now
gtgmmiloms - got to go my mum is looking over my shoulder
gtgn - got to go now
gtgp - got to go pee
gtgpp - got to go pee pee
gtgtb - got to go to bed
gtgtpirio - got to go the price is right is on
gtgtwn - Got to go to work now

gth - go to hell
gtha - go the hell away
gthb - go to hell b***h
gthmf - go to hell mothaf**ka
gtho - get the hell out
gthu - grow the heck up
gthyfah - a
gtk - good to know
gtm - giggling to myself
gtn - getting
gtp - Got to pee
gtr - Got to run
gts - going to school
gtsy - good to see you
gttp - get to the point
gtty - good talking to you
gu - grow up
gu2i - get used to it
gud - good
gudd - good
gui - graphical user interface
gurl - girl
gurlz - girls
guru - expert
gw - good work
gwijd - guess what i just did
gwm - gay white male
gwork - good work
gwrk - good work
gws - get well soon
gwytose - go waste your time on someone else
gy - gay
gyal - girl
gypo - Get Your Penis Out
h&k - hugs and kisses
h*r - homestar runner
h+k - hugs and kisses
h.o - hold on
h/e - However
h/mo - homo

h/o - hold on
h/u - hold up
h/w - homework
h2 - Halo 2
h2gtb - have to go to the bathroom
h2o - water
h2sys - hope to see you soon
h3y - hey
h4kz0r5 - hackers
h4x - Hacks
h4x0r - hacker
h4xor - hacker
h4xr - hacker
h4xrz - hackers
h4xx0rz - hacker
h4xxor - hacker
h8 - hate
h80r - hater
h82sit - hate to say it
h83r - hater
h8ed - hated
h8er - hater
h8r - hater
h8red - Hatred
h8s - hates
h8t - hate
h8t0r - hater
h8t3r - hater
h8te - hate
h8tr - hater
h8u - I Hate You
h9 - Husband in Room
habt - how about this
hafta - have to
hagd - have a good day
hagl - have a great life
hagn - have a good night
hago - have a good one
hags - have a great summer
hai - hello

hait - hate
hak - here's a kiss
hakas - have a kick a** summer
hammrd - hammered
han - how about now
hau - How Are You
hav - have
havnt - haven't
hawf - Husband and Wife forever
hawt - hot
hawtie - hottie
hax - Hacks
hax0r - hacker
hax0red - hacked
hax0rz - Hackers
haxer - Hacker
haxor - hacker
haxoring - hacking
haxors - hackers
haxorz - hackers
haxxor - hacker
haxxzor - Hacker
haxz0r - Hacker
haxzor - hacker
hayd - how are you doing
hb - hurry back
hb4b - hoes before bros
hbd - happy birthday
hbic - head b***h in charge
hbii - how big is it
hbu - how about you
hby - how about you
hc - how come
hcbt1 - he could be the one
hcib - how can it be
hcihy - how can I help you
hdop - Help Delete Online Predators
hdu - how dare you
hdydi - How do you do it
hdydt - how did you do that

heh - haha
hella - very
heya - hey
heyt - hate
heyy - hello
heyya - hello
hf - have fun
hfn - Hell f**king no
hfs - holy f**king s**t!
hfsbm - holy f**king s**t batman
hfwt - have fun with that
hg - HockeyGod
hght - height
hhiad - holy hole in a doughnut
hhiadb - Holy Hole in a Donut Batman
hhok - Ha Ha Only Kidding
hhyb - how have you been
hi2u - hello
hi2u2 - hello to you too
hiet - height
hiik - Hell If I Know
hijack - start an off topic discussion
hith - how in the hell
hiw - husband is watching
hiya - hello
hiybbprqag - copying somebody else's search results
hj - hand job
hl - Half-Life
hl2 - Half-Life 2
hla - Hot lesbian action
hlb - horny little b*****d
hld - hold
hldn - hold on
hldon - hold on
hll - Hell
hlm - he loves me
hlo - hello
hlp - help
hly - holy
hlysht - Holy s**t

hmb - hold me back
hmewrk - homework
hmfic - head mother f**ker in charge
hml - hate my life
hmoj - holy mother of jesus
hmu - Hit Me Up
hmul - Hit me up later
hmus - Hit me up sometime
hmw - homework
hmwk - homework
hmwrk - Homework
hng - horny net geek
hngry - hungry
hnic - head n****r in charge
ho - hold on
hoas - Hang on a second
hoay - how old are you
hoh - head of household
hom - home
homey - Friend
homie - good friend
homo - homosexual
hoopty - broke down automobile
hott - hot
howdey - hello
howz - hows
hpb - high ping b*****d
hpoa - Hot Piece of a**
hppy - Happy
hpy - happy
hpybdy - happy birthday
hr - hour
hre - here
hrny - horny
hrs - hours
hru - how are you
hrud - how are you doing
hs - headshot
hsd - high school dropout
hsik - how should i know

hsr - homestar runner
hss - horse s**t and splinters
hswm - Have Sex With me
ht - Heard Through
htc - hit the cell
htf - how the f**k
htfu - Hurry the f**k up
hth - hope that helps
hthu - Hurry the hell up
htr - hater
http - hyper text transfer protocol
hu - Hey you
hubby - husband
hud - Heads Up Display
huggle - hug and cuddle
hugz - hugs
hun - honey
hv - have
hve - have
hvnt - haven't
hw - homework
hw/hw - help me with homework
hwg - here we go
hwga - here we go again
hwik - how would i know
hwk - homework
hwmbo - he who must be obeyed
hwmnbn - he who must not be named
hwms - hot wild monkey sex
hwu - hey what's up
hwz - how is
hxc - hardcore
hy - hell yeah
hyb - how you been
hyg - here you go
hyk - how you know
i <3 u - I love you
i c - i see
i8 - alright
i8u - i hate you

i<3 u - i love you
i<3u - I love you
iab - I Am Bored
iafh - I Am f**king Hot
iafi - I am from India
iag - it's all good
iah - i am horny
iai - i am interested
ianabs - I am not a brain surgeon
ianacl - I am not a copyright lawyer
ianal - I am not a lawyer
ianalb - I am not a lawyer, but..
ianars - I am not a rocket scientist
ians - I am Not Sure
ianyl - I am not your lawyer
iap - I Am Pissed
iasb - i am so bored
iaspfm - i am sorry please forgive me
iatb - I am the best
iateu - i hate you
iavb - i am very bored
iaw - In Another Window
iawtc - I agree with this comment
iawtp - I agree with this post
iawy - I agree with you
ib - I'm back
ibbl - I'll be back later
ibcd - Idiot between chair & desk
ibs - Internet b***h Slap
ibt - I'll be there
ibtl - In Before The Lock
ibw - I'll be waiting
ic - I see
icb - I can't believe
icbi - i can't believe it
icbiwoop - I chuckled, but it was out of pity.
icbt - i can't believe that
icbu - I can't believe you
icbyst - i cant believe you said that
iccl - I could care less

icgup - I can give you pleasure
icic - I See. I See
icp - insane clown posse
icr - I can't rememer
icsrg - I can still reach Google
ictrn - I can't talk right now
icty - i can't tell you
icu - i see you
icudk - in case you didn't know
icup - i see you pee
icw - I care why?
icwudt - I see what you did there
icwum - I see what you mean
icydk - in csae you didn't know
icydn - in case you didn't know
icymi - in case you missed it
id10t - idiot
idbtwdsat - I don't believe they would do such a thing
idby - I Don't Believe You
idc - I don't care
iddi - I didn't do it
idec - I don't even care
idek - I don't even know
idfc - i don't f**king care
idfk - i don't f**king know
idfts - I don't f**king think so
idgac - i don't give a crap
idgad - I don't give a d**n
idgaf - i don't give a f**k
idgaff - I don't give a flying f**k
idgafs - I don't give a f**king s**t
idgara - I don't give a rat's a**
idgas - i don't give a s**t
idgi - I don't get it
idjit - idiot
idk - I don't know
idkbibt - I don't know but I've Been Told
idke - I don't know ethier
idkh - I don't know how
idkh2s - i don't know how to spell

idkt - I don't know that
idkw - I don't know why
idkwiwdwu - I don't know what I would do without you
idkwts - I don't know what to say
idkwurta - I don't know what you are talking about.
idkwym - I don't know what you mean
idky - I don't know you
idkyb - i don't know why but
idkymb2 - I didn't know yoru mom blogs too
idl - I don't like
idli - I don't like it
idlu - i don't like you
idly - I don't like you
idlyitw - i don't like you in that way
idm - I don't mind
idn - i don't know
idnk - i don't know
idno - i do not know
idntk - i dont need to know
idnwths - i do not want to have sex
idonno - i do not know
idop - it depends on price
idot - idiot
idr - I don't remember
idrc - i don't really care
idrfk - I don't really f**king know
idrgaf - I don't really give a f**k
idrk - i don't really know
idrts - I don't really think so
idsw - i don't see why
idtis - I don't think I should
idtkso - i don't think so
idts - i don't think so
idunno - i do not know
iduwym - I don't understand what you mean.
idw2 - I don't want to
idw2n - i don't want to know
idwk - I don't wanna know
idwt - i don't want to
idwtg - I don't want to go

idyat - idiot
iebkac - issue exists between keyboard and chair
ietf - internet engineering task force
iff - if and only if
ifhu - I f**king hate you
ifhy - i f**king hate you
iflu - i f**king love you
ifthtb - i find that hard to belive
ifttt - if this then that
ifwis - I forgot what I said
ig - I guess
ig2g - I got to go
ig5oi - I got 5 on it
igahp - I've got a huge penis
igalboc - I've got a lovely bunch of cocnuts
igg - i gotta go
ight - alright
igkymfa - I'm gonna kick your mother f**king a**
igs - I guess so
igt - I Got This
igtg - i've got to go
igtgt - I got to go tinkle
igtkya - im going to kick your a**
igu - i give up
igyb - I Got Your Back
ih - it happens
ih2gp - I have to go pee
ih2p - i'll have to pa**
ih8 - i hate
ih8mls - I hate my little sister
ih8p - I hate parents
ih8tu - i hate you
ih8u - I hate you
ih8usm - i hate you so much
ih8y - I hate you
ihac - I have a customer
ihat3u - I hate you
ihistr - i hope i spelled that right
ihiwydt - I hate it when you do that
ihml - I hate my life

ihmp - i hate my parents
ihnc - i have no clue
ihnfc - I have no f**king clue
ihni - i have no idea
iht - I heard that
ihtfp - I hate this f**king place
ihtgttbwijd - I have to go to the bathroom, wait I just did.
ihtp - I Have To Poop
ihtsm - i hate this so much
ihtutbr - I have to use the bathroom
ihu - I hate you
ihurg - i hate your guts
ihusb - i hate you so bad
ihusfm - i hate you so f**king much
ihusm - i hate you so much
ihy - i hate you
ihya - i hate you all
ihysm - I hate you so much
ihysmrn - i hate you so much right now
iigh - alright
iight - alright
iiok - is it okay
iirc - if I recall correctly
iistgtbtipi - If It Sounds Too Good To Be True It Probably Is
iit - is it tight
iitywimwybmad - if I tell you what it means will you buy me a drink
iitywybmad - if I tell you, will you buy me a drink?
iiuc - if I understand correctly
iiw2 - is it web 2.0?
iiwii - it is what it is
ij - indide joke
ijaf - it's just a fact
ijcomk - i just came on my keyboard
ijdk - I just don't know
ijdl - I just died laughing
ijeomk - I just ejaculated on my keybord
ijf - i just farted
ijgl - I just got laid
ijit - idiot

ijk - I'm Just kidding
ijp - Internet job posting
ijpmp - I just peed my pants
ijpms - I just pissed myself
ijr - i just remembered
ijsabomomcibstg - I just saved a bunch of money on my car insurance by switching to GARIVS
ik - i know
iki - i know it
ikm - I know man
ikr - I know really
ikt - i knew that
ikwud - I know what you did
ikwum - I know what you meant
ikwyl - I know where you live
ikwym - i know what you mean
ilbbaicnl - I like big butts and I can not lie
ilbcnu - i'll be seeing you
ilcul8r - I'll see you later
ilhsm - i love him/her so much
ili - i love it
ilk2fku - I would like to f**k you
ilml - I Love My Life
ilms - I love my self
ilotibinlirl - I'm laughing on the internet, but I'm not laughing in real life
ilshipmp - I laughed so hard I peed my pants
iltf - i love to f**k
ilu - I love you
ilu2 - I love you too
iluaaf - i love you as a friend
ilulafklc - I love you like a fat kid loves cake.
ilum - i love you more
ilusfm - I love you so f**king much
ilusm - I love you So much
iluvm - I Love You Very Much
iluvu - i love you
iluvya - i love you
iluwamh - i love you with all my heart
ilvu - i love you

ily - i love you
ily2 - i love you too
ily4e - i love you forever
ily4ev - i love you forever
ilyaas - I Love You As A Sister
ilyal - I like you a lot
ilyb - i love you b***h
ilybby - i love you baby
ilybtid - I Love You But Then I Don't
ilyf - I'll Love You Forever
ilygsm - i love you guys so much
ilykthnxbai - i love you k thanks bye
ilyl - i love you loads
ilylab - I love you like a brother
ilylabf - I love you like a best friend
ilylafklc - i love you like a fat kid loves cake
ilylas - i love you like a sister
ilylc - i love you like crazy
ilym - i love you more
ilymtyk - i love you more than you know
ilymtylm - i love you more than you love me
ilysfm - i love you so f**king much
ilysfmb - i love you so f**king much baby
ilysm - i love you so much
ilysmih - i love you so much it hurts
ilysmm - i love you so much more
ilysmydek - I Love You So Much You Don't Even Know
ilysvm - i love you so very much
ilyvm - i love you very much
ilywamh - I love you with all my heart
im - Instant Message
im'd - instant messaged
im26c4u - I am too sexy for you
ima - I am a
imao - in my arrogant opinion
imb - I am back
imcdo - in my conceited dogmatic opinion
imed - instant messaged
imfao - In My f**king Arrogant Opinion
imfo - in my f**king opinion

imh - I am here
imhbco - In my humble but correct opinion
imhe - in my humble experience
imho - in my humble opinion
imm - instant message me
imma - I'm going to
imnerho - In my not even remotely humble opinion
imnl - I'm not laughing
imnshmfo - In My Not So Humble Mother f**king Opinion
imnsho - in my not so humble opinion
imo - in my opinion
imoo - in my own opinion
impo - In My Personal Opinion
impov - in my point of view
imsb - i am so bored
imsry - I am sorry
imtaw - it may take a while
imts - I meant to say
imu - i miss you
imusm - I miss you so much
imvho - in my very humble opinion
imwtk - Inquiring minds want to know
imy - I miss you
imy2 - i miss you to
imya - i miss you already
imysfm - i miss you so f**king much
in2 - into
inb4 - in before
inbd - it's no big deal
incld - include
incrse - increase
ind2p - I need to pee
indie - independent
inef - it's not even funny
inet - internet
inh - I need help
inho - in my honest opinion
inhwh - I need homework help
init - isn't it
inmp - it's not my problem

innit - isn't it
ino - I know
instagib - instant kill
instakill - instant kill
intarwebs - internet
intel - intelligence
interweb - internet
intpftpotm - I nominate this post for the post of the month
inttwmf - I am Not Typing This With My Fingers
invu - I envy you
ioh - I'm out of here
iois - Indicators of Interest
iokiya - it's ok if you are
ionno - I don't know
iono - I don't know
iotd - image of the day
iou - i owe you
iow - in other words
ioya - I'd Own Your a**
ioyk - if only you knew
ip - internet protocol
irc - internet relay chat
irdc - I really don't care
irdgaf - i really don't give a f**k
irdk - I really don't know
irgtgbtw - I've really got to get back to work
irhtgttbr - I really have to go to the bathroom
irhy - i really hate you
irl - in real life
irly - I really love you
irt - in reply to
irtf - I'll return the favor
is2g - i swear to god
isb - I'm so bored.
isbya - im sorry but you asked
isd - internet slang dictionary
ise - internal server error
isfly - i so f**king love you
isg - I speak geek
ishii - i see how it is

isianmtu - I swear I am not making this up
isj - inside joke
iso - In Search Of
isp - internet service provider
iss - im so sorry
istr - I seem to remember
istwfn - I stole this word from noslang.com
iswydt - i see what you did there
ita - I Totally Agree
itb - in the butt
itc - in that case
itd - in the dark
ite - alright
itk - in the know
itn - I think not
itt - in this thread
ityltk - I thought you'd like to know
itz - it's
itzk - it's ok
iucmd - if you catch my drift
iukwim - if you know what i mean
iunno - I don't know
iuno - i dunno
ive - i have
iw2f - i want to f**k
iw2fu - i want to f**k you
iw2mu - I want to meet you
iwaa - It was an accident
iwbrbl@r - I will be right back later
iwc - In Which Case
iwfusb - i wanna f**k you so bad
iwfy - I want to f**k you
iwfybo - i will f**k your brains out
iwg - it was good
iwhi - I would hit it
iwhswu - I want to have sex with you
iwjk - i was just kidding
iwk - I wouldn't know
iwlu4e - I will love you for ever
iwmu - i will miss you

iwmy - i will miss you
iws - i want sex
iwsn - i want sex now
iwsul8r - I will see you later
iwtfu - i want to f**k you
iwtfy - i want to f**k you
iwthswy - i want to have sex with you
iwtly - i want to love you
iwu - i want you
iwuwh - i wish you were here
iwy - i want you
iwyb - I want your body
iwyn - I want you now
iwythmb - i want you to have my baby
iyam - if you ask me
iyc - if you can
iyd - In Your Dreams
iydhantsdsaaa - If you don't have anything nice to say don't say anything at all
iydmma - if you don't mind me asking
iyf - In your face
iyflg - If You're Feeling Less Generous
iygm - if you get me
iykwim - if you know what I mean
iym - I am your man
iyo - in your opinion
iyq - I like you
iyss - if you say so
iyswim - if you see what I mean
iywt - if you want to
iz - is
j-c - just chilling
j/a - Just Asking
j/c - just curious
j/j - just joking
j/k - just kidding
j/o - jackoff
j/p - just playing
j/s - just saying
j/t - just talking

j/w - just wondering
j00 - you
j00r - your
j2bs - just to be sure
j2c - just too cute
j2f - just too funny
j2luk - just to let you know
j2lyk - just to let you know
j4f - just for fun
j4g - just for grins
j4l - just for laughs
j4u - just for you
jalaudlm - just as long as you don't leave me
jas - just a second
jb - jailbait
jbu - just between us
jc - just curious
jcam - just checking away message
jcath - Just chilling at the house
jdfi - Just f**king do it
jebus - Jesus
jeomk - Just ejaculated on my keyboard
jf - just fooling
jfc - Jesus f**king Christ
jfdi - Just f**king Do It!
jff - just for fun
jfg - just for giggles
jfgi - just f**king google it
jfi - just forget it
jfj - jump for joy
jfk - Just f**king kidding
jfl - just for laughs
jflts - just felt like typing something
jfn - just for now
jfo - just f**k off
jfr - Just for reference
jftr - just for the record
jfu - just for you
jfwy - just f**king with you
jg2h - just go to hell

jgiyn - Just google it you noob
jgtfooh - just get the f**k out of here
jh - Just hanging
jhm - just hold me
jho - just hanging out
jic - just in case
jit - just in time
jizz - semen
jj - just joking
jj/k - just joking
jja - just joking around
jk - just kidding
jka - just kidding around
jking - joking
jkl - just kidding loser
jklol - Just Kidding Laughing Out Loud
jkn - joking
jks - jokes
jkz - jokes
jlma - just leave me alone
jlt - just like that
jm - Just Messing
jma - just messing around
jml - just my luck
jmo - just my opinion
jms - just making sure
jom - just one minuite
joo - you
jooc - just out of curiosity
jooce - Juice
joor - your
jp - just playing
js - just saying
jsa - just stop already
jsing - just saying
jst - just
jsuk - just so you know
jsun - Just so you know
jsut - just
jsyk - Just so you know

jsyn - just so you know
jtay - just thinking about you
jtbs - Just To Be Sure
jtc - Join the club
jtfo - joke the f**k out
jtluk - just to let you know
jtlyk - just to let you know
jtoi - just thought of it
jtol - just thinking out loud
jttsiowctw - just testing to see if other websites copy this word
jtty - just to tell you
jtumltk - just thought you might like to know
jtwii - just the way it is.
jtwiw - just the way it was.
jtyltk - just thought you'd like to know
jtysk - just thought you should know
jumping the couch - acting strange
jus - just
juss - just
juz - just
juzt - just
jw - just wondering
jw2k - just wanted to know
jwas - just wait a second
jwtlyk - Just wanted to let you know
jyfihp - jam your finger in her p***y
k - ok
k3wl - cool
ka - Kick a**
kafn - kill all f**king noobs
kah - kisses and hugs
kaw - kick a** work
kay - okay
kb - KiloBite
kcco - keep calm chive on
kek - laughing out loud
kewel - cool
kewl - cool
kfc - kentucky fried chicken
khitbash - kick her in the box and shove her

khuf - know how you feel
kia - Killed In Action
kib - okay, im back
kic - keep it clean
kicks - sneakers
kig - keep it going
kiled - killed
kinda - kind of
kir - kid in room
kis - keep it simple
kisa - knight in shining armor
kit - keep in touch
kitfo - knock it the f**k off
kitteh - kitten
kiu - Keep it up
kiwf - Kill It With Fire
kk - ok
kkk - ku klux klan
kkthnxbye - okay thanks bye
kky - kinky
kl - cool
km - kiss me
kma - kiss my a**
kmag - kiss my a** goodbye
kmao - kick my a** off
kmb - kiss my butt
kmfa - kiss my f**king a**
kmhba - kiss my hairy big a**
kmn - kill me now
kmp - kill me please
kmsl - killing myself laughing
kmswl - killing myself with laughter
knackered - drunk
knewb - new player
knn - f**k your mother
kno - know
knw - know
ko - knock out
kol - kiss on lips
koo - cool

kool - cool
kos - kid over shoulder
kotc - kiss on the cheek
kotl - kiss on the lips
kotor - Knights of the old republic
kots - keep on talking s**t
kpc - keeping parents clueless
ks - kill steal
kss - kiss
kssd - kissed
kt - keep talking
ktc - kill the cat
ktfo - knocked the f**k out
kthanxbi - Okay, thanks. Bye.
kthnxbai - Okay, thanks, bye
kthnxbye - Okay, thanks, bye
kthx - ok, thank you
kthxbai - ok thanks bye!
kthxbi - ok, thank you, goodbye
kthxbye - ok, thank you, goodbye
kthxbye - ok, thank you, goodbye
kthxgb - ok thanks goodbye
kthxmn - Ok Thanks Man
kthz - ok thanks
ktnx - Okay and Thanks
kuhl - cool
kul - cool
kute - cute
kutgw - Keep Up The good Work
kuwl - cool
kwik - quick
kwim - Know What I Mean
kwis - Know what I'm saying?
kwit - quit
kwiz - quiz
kwl - cool
kwtsds - Kiss where the sun don't shine
kyag - Kiss Your a** Goodbye
kyfag - kiss your f**king a** goodbye
kyfc - keep your fingers crossed

kyko - keep your knickers on
kys - kill yourself
10lz - laugh out loud
12 - learn to
12m - listening to music
12ms - laughing to myself
12p - learn to play
12r - Learn to read
1337 - elite
133t - elite
14m3rz - lamers
18 - late
184skool - late for school
18a - later
18er - later
18ers - Later
18r - see you later
18rs - laters
18rz - later
18s - later
18t - later
18ta - later
18ter - later
18tr - later
l@u - laughing at you
laff - laugh
lafs - love at first sight
lak - love and kisses
lal - laughing a little
lalol - lots and lots of laughs
lam - leave a message
lamf - like a motherf**ker
lan - local area network
lappy - Laptop
larp - live action role-play
lasb - Lame a** Stupid b***h
lat - laugh at that
lata - later
lates - later
latn - laugh at the newbs

latr - Later
latwttb - laughing all the way to the bank
lau - laugh at you
lawd - lord
lawl - lauging out loud with a southern drawl
lawl'd - laughed out loud
lawled - laughed out loud
lawls - laughing out loud with a southern drawl
lawlz - laughing out loud with a southern drawl
lazer - laser
lazor - laser
lbh - let's be honest
lbnr - laughing but not really
lbo - laughing butt off
lbr - little boy's room
lbvs - laughing but very serious
lcsnpc - low cost small notebook personal computer
ldr - Long-distance relationship
lee7 - elite
leet - elite
legit - legitimate
leik - like
leme - let me
lemme - let me
lesbo - lesbian
less than 3 - love
less than three - love
lez - Lesbian
lezbean - lesbian
lezbo - lesbian
lezzzie - lesbian
lf - looking for
lf1m - Looking for one more
lf2m - looking for 2 more
lfg - Looking for group
lfl - let's f**k later
lfm - looking for mate
lfnar - laughing for no aparent reason
lfp - looking for p***y
lfr - Laughing for real

lgb - lesbian/gay/bisexual
lgbnaf - lets get butt naked and f**k
lgbtq - Lesbien, Gay, Bisexual, Transgender and Queer.
lgf - little green footballs
lggd - let's go get drunk
lgn - link goes nowhere
lgo - life goes on
lgot - let's go out tonight
lgr - little girls room
lgs - let's go shopping!
lhao - laughing her a** off
lhs - lets have sex
lhsrn - let's have sex right now
lic - like i care
liec - like i even care
liek - like
liekz - likes
lifo - last in first out
ligaff - like I give a flying f**k
ligafs - like I give a flying s**t
ligas - like I give a s**t
lih - Laugh in head
liita - love is in the air
lik - like
lil - little
lim - Like it Matters
limh - laugh in my head
liol - laugh insanely out loud
lirl - laughing in real life
liu - Look It Up
liv - live
liyf - laughing in your face
lj - live journal
lk - like
lke - like
llab - Laughing like a b***h.
llap - live long and prosper
llc - laughing like crazy
llf - laugh like f**k
llol - literally laughing out loud

lltnt - live like theres no tomorrow
lm4aq - Let's meet for a quickie.
lma - leave me alone
lmamf - leave me alone mother f**ker
lmao - laughing my a** off
lmaol - laughing my a** out loud
lmaomtoaoa - Laugh my a** off many times over and over again
lmaonade - laughing my a** off
lmaool - laughing my a** off out loud
lmaootf - Laughing my a** off on the floor
lmaorof - Laughing my a** off Rolling on the floor
lmaorotf - laughing my a** off rolling on the floor
lmaowrotf - Laughing my a** of while rolling on the floor
lmaowtntpm - laughing my a** off whilst trying not to piss myself
lmaoxh - laughing my a** off extremely hard
lmap - leave me alone please
lmb - lick my balls
lmbao - laughing my black a** off
lmbfwao - laughing my big fat white a** off
lmbo - laughing my butt off
lmcao - laughing my crazy a** off
lmclao - laughing my cute little a** off
lmd - Lick My d**k
lmfao - laughing my f**king a** off
lmfbo - laugh my f**king butt off
lmffao - laughing my f**king fat a** off
lmffo - Laughing my f**king face off
lmfho - laughing my f**king head off
lmfo - laughing my face off
lmfpo - laughing my f**king p***y off
lmfr - Lets Meet For Real
lmfto - laughing my f**kin tits off
lmg - let me guess
lmgdao - Laughing My God d**n a** Off
lmgtfy - Let me Google that for you
lmhao - laughing my hairy a** off
lmho - laughing my heiny off
lmip - LETS MEET IN PERSON
lmirl - Let's meet in real life
lmk - let me know

lmks - Let Me Know Soon
lmkwut - let me know what you think
lml - love my life
lmmfao - laughing my mother f**king a** off
lmmfaos - laughing my mother f**king a** off silly
lmmfas - laugh my mother f**kin a** off
lmmffao - laughing my mother f**king fat a** off
lmo - Leave Me One
lmoao - Laughing my Other a** Off
lmp - lick my p***y
lmpo - laughing my panties off
lms - leave me some
lmsao - laughing my sexy a** off
lmso - laughing my socks off
lmtd - limited
lmtfa - leave me the f**k alone
lmto - laughing my tits off
lmtus - let me tell you something
lmty - laughing more than you
lmvo - laugh my vagina off
ln - last name
lnk - Link
lobfl - Laugh Out Bloody f**king Loud
lof - Laughing on floor
lofi - uncool
lofl - laugh out f**king loud
loflmao - laying on floor laughing my a** off
loi - laughing on the inside
lol - laughing out loud
lol'd - laughed out loud
lol2u - Laugh out loud to you
lol@u - Laugh out loud at you
lolarotf - laughing out loud and rolling on the floor
lolaw - laugh out loud at work
lolcano - laugh out loud
lolci - laughing out loud, crying inside
lolcity - the whole city laughs out loud
lold - laughed out loud
lolees - laugh out loud
lolerz - laugh out loud

lolf - lots of love forever
lolin - laughing out loud
lolio - laugh out loud I own
lollam - Laughing Out Loud Like A Maniac
lollercaust - an extreme event of hilarity
lollercoaster - laugh out loud (a lot)
lollerskates - laughing out loud
lolm - laugh out loud man
loln - laught out loud... not
lolngs - laghing out loud never gonna stop
lolocost - laugh out loud
lolol - saying "lol" out loud
lololz - laugh out loud
lolpimp - Laughing out loud peeing in my pants
lolq - laugh out loud quietly
lolrof - Laughing out loud while rolling on the floor.
lolrotf - laughing out loud rolling on the floor
lols - laugh out loud
lolvq - laugh out loud very quietly
lolwtime - laughing out loud with tears in my eyes
lolz - laugh out loud
lomg - like oh my god
loml - love of my life
lomy - love of my life
loomm - laughing out of my mind
lorl - laugh out real loud
lorrl - laugh out really really loud
lotf - laughing on the floor
loti - laughing on the inside
lotr - lord of the rings
lov - love
lovu - love you
loxen - laughing out loud
loxxen - laughing out loud
lozer - loser
lpb - low ping b*****d
lpiaw - Large Penis is always welcome
lpms - life pretty much sucks
lq - Laughing Quietly
lq2m - laughing quietly to myself

lqtm - Laugh quietly to myself
lqtms - Laughing quietly to myself
lqts - laughing quietly to self
lrfl - Laughing really f**king loud
lrh - laughing really hard
lrqtms - laughing really quietly to myself
lrt - last retweet
lsfw - Less Safe For Work
lshic - laughing so hard i'm crying
lshid - laugh so hard i die
lshipmp - Laughing so Hard I Piss My Pants
lshismp - laughed so hard I s**t my pants
lshiwms - laughing so hard I wet myself
lshmson - laughing so hard milk shot out nose
lshrn - laughing so hard right now
lsmih - laughing so much it hurts
lsr - loser
lsudi - Lets see you do it
lt - long time
ltb - looking to buy
lthtt - laughing too hard to type
ltip - laughting until I puke
ltm - listen to me
ltmq - Laugh To Myself Quietly
ltms - Laughing to my self
ltnc - Long time no see
ltns - long time no see
ltnsoh - Long time, no see or hear
ltnt - long time no talk
ltp - Lay the pipe
ltr - later
lttpot - laughing to the point of tears
ltw - Lead The Way
ltywl - love the way you lie
lu2 - love you too
lu2d - love you to death
lu4l - love you for life
lub - laugh under breath
luf - love
luff - Love

lug - lesbian until graduation
luk - look
lukin - looking
lul - love you lots
lulab - Love you like a brother
lulas - Love You Like a Sister
lulz - Laughing out loud.
lurker - one who reads but doesn't reply
lurve - love
luser - user who is a loser
lusm - love you so much
luv - love
luver - lover
luvuvm - love you very much
luvv - love
luzar - Loser
lv - love
lve - Love
lvl - level
lvn - loving
lvr - lover
lvya - love you
lwih - look what I have
lwn - last week's news
ly - love you
ly2 - love you to
lya - love you always
lyaab - Love you as a brother
lyaaf - Love you as a friend
lyao - laugh your a** off
lybo - laugh your butt off
lyf - life
lyfao - laughing your f**king a** off
lyfe - life
lyk - like
lyk3 - like
lyke - like
lyl - love you lots
lylab - love you like a brother
lylaba - love you like a brother always

lylad - love you like a dad
lylafklc - love you like a fat kid loves cake
lylam - love you like a mom
lylas - I love you like a sister
lylasa - love you like a sister always
lylno - Love you like no other
lyls - love you lots
lymi - love you mean it
lysfm - love you so f**king much
lysm - love you so much
lyt - love you too
lyvm - love you very much
lzer - laser
lzr - loser
m - am
m$ - Microsoft
m$wxp - Microsoft Windows XP
m&d - mom and dad
m'kay - okay
m.i.a - Missing In Action
m.o - makeout
m/b - maybe
m/f - male or female
m2 - me too
m3 - me
m473s - friends
m473z - friends
m4f - male for female
m4m - male for male
m8 - friend
m84l - mate for life
m8s - mates
m8t - mate
m8t's - friends
m9 - mine
mabby - maybe
mabe - Maybe
mah - my
mai - my
mao - my a** off

marvy - marvelous
masterb8 - masterbate
mastrb8 - masturbate.
mayb - maybe
mayte - mate
mb - my bad
mbf - my best friend
mbfal - my best friend and lover
mbhsm - My Boobs Hurt So Much
mbl8r - Maybe Later
mcds - mcdonalds
mcs - My computer sucks
mcse - Microsoft Certified Systems Engineer
me2 - me too
meatcurtain - woman's private parts
meatspace - the real world
meeh - me
mego - my eyes glaze over
meh - whatever
messg - message
mf - motherf**ker
mf2f4sx - meet face to face for sex
mfa - mother f**king a**h**e
mfah - motherf**king a**h**e
mfao - my f**king a** off
mfb - mother f**king b***h
mfg - merge from current
mfkr - motherf**ker
mflfs - married female looking for sex
mfr - motherf**ker
mfw - my face when
mgiwjsdchmw - my girlfriend is watching jeff so don't call her my wife
mhh - my head hurts
mhm - Yes
mho - My Humble Opinion
mia - Missing In Action
mic - microphone
miid - my internet is down
milf - Mom i'd like to f**k

miltf - Mom I'd like to f**k
min - minute
mins - minutes
miq - make it quick
mir - mom in room
mirl - meet in real life
misc. - miscellaneous
miself - myself
mite - might
miw - mom is watching
miwnlf - mom I would not like to f**k.
mk - mmm....ok
mkay - ok
mlc - mid life crisis
mle - emily
mlia - my life is amazing
mlod - mega laugh out loud of doom
mlp - my little pony
mmamp - Meet me at my place
mmas - meet me after school
mmatc - meet me around the corner
mmatp - meet me at the park
mmbocmb - message me back or comment me back
mmd - make my day
mmiw - my mom is watching
mmk - umm, ok
mml - making me laugh
mml8r - meet me later
mmlfs - married man looking for sex
mmmkay - okay
mmo - Massive Multiplayer Online
mmt - meet me there
mmtyh - My mom thinks you're hot
mmw - making me wet
mngmt - management
mngr - manager
mnm - eminem
mnt - More next time
mobo - motherboard
mof - matter of fact

mofo - mother f**ker
moh - Medal Of Honor
mohaa - Medal of Honor Allied Assult
mol - more or less
mompl - moment please
moobs - man boobs
mor - more
morf - male or female
moro - tomorrow
mos - mom over shoulder
moss - member of same sex
motarded - more retarded
motd - message of the day
motos - member of the opposite sex
mpaw - my parents are watching
mpbis - most popular boy in school
mpd - Multiple Personality Disorder
mpgis - most popular girl in school
mph - miles per hour
mpih - my penis is hard
mpty - more power to you
mrau - message received and understood
msf - male seeking female
msg - message
msgs - messages
msh - Me so horny
msibo - my side is busting open
msie - microsoft's internet explorer
msm - main stream media
msmd - monkey see - monkey do
msngr - messenger
mssg - message
msv - Microsoft Vista
mtc - more to come
mtf - More to Follow
mtfbwu - may the force be with you
mtfbwy - May the Force be with you
mtg - Meeting
mtherfker - mother f**ker
mthrfkr - mother f**ker

mtl - more than likely
mtr - matter
mtrfkr - motherf**ker
mty - empty
mu - miss you
mudda - mother
mul - miss you lots
musiq - music
musm - Miss You So Much
mutha - mother
muve - multi-user virtual environment
muvva - mother
muzik - music
mw2 - modern warfare 2
mw3 - Modern Warfare 3
mwah - kiss
mwf - Married White Female
mwsmirl - maybe we should meet in real life
myaly - miss you and love you
myfb - mind your f**king business
myke - man-dyke
myn - mine
myob - mind your own business
myodb - mind your own d**n business
myofb - mind your own f**king business
mypl - my young padawan learner
mysm - Miss you so much
myspce - myspace
mmorpg - massively multiplayer online role playing game
n - and
n e - any
n/a - not applicable
n/a/s/l - name, age, sex location
n/c - no comment
n/m - nevermind
n/n - nickname
n/o - no offense
n/t - no text
n00b - newbie
n00bs - newbies

n00dz - nudes
n00s - news
n1 - nice one
n199312 - african american
n1994 - african american
n2 - into
n2b - not too bad
n2bb - nice to be back
n2br - not to be rude
n2g - Not too good
n2m - not too much
n2mh - not too much here
n2mhbu - not too much how about you?
n2mhjc - not too much here just chillin
n2mu - not too much, you?
n2n - need to know
n2p - need to pee
n64 - Nintendo 64
n8v - native
na - not applicable
na4w - not appropriate for work
naa - not at all
nade - grenade
nafc - Not Appropriate for Children
nafkam - Not Away From Keyboard Any More
naft - Not A f**king Thing
nafta - North American Free Trade Agreement
nah - no
namh - not at my house
nao - Not As Often
natch - naturally
natm - not at the minute
naw - no
naw-t - Naughty
nawidt - never again will i do that
nawt - not
naww - no
nayl - in a while
nb - not bad
nb,p - nothing bad, parents

nba - national basketball association
nbd - no big deal
nbdy - nobody
nc - not cool
ncaa - National Collegiate Athletic Association
ncs - no crap sherlock
nd - and
ndit - No details in thread
ndn - indian
nds - Nintendo DS
ne - any
ne1 - anyone
neday - any day
nedn - any day now
nefing - anything
neida - any idea
nekkid - naked
nemore - Anymore
nes - Nintendo Entertainment System
nethin - anything
nething - anything
neva - never
nevah - never
nevar - Never
nevarz - never
nevm - never mind
nevr - never
newais - Anyways
neway - anyway
neways - anyways
newayz - anyways
newb - someone who is new
newbie - new player
newez - anyways
nf - not funny
nfbsk - not for british school kids
nfc - no f**king clue
nfd - no f**king deal
nff - not f**king fair
nfi - no f**king idea

nfr - not for real
nfs - not for sale
nft - no further text
nfw - no f**king way
ng - nice game
ngaf - nobody gives a f**k
ngl - Not Gonna Lie
nh - nice hand
nhatm - not here at the moment
ni - no idea
ni994 - n***a
nib - new in box
nic - Network Interface Card
nif - non internet friend
nifoc - naked in front of computer
nifok - naked in front of keyboard
nigysob - now I've got you son of a b***h
nimby - not in my backyard
nin - no its not
nip - nothing in particular
nips - nipples
nite - night
nizzle - n****r
nj - Nice job
njoy - enjoy
njp - nice job partner
nk - no kidding
nkt - never knew that
nld - nice lay down
nm - not much
nm u - not much, you
nmbr - number
nme - enemy
nmf - not my fault
nmfp - not my f**king problem
nmh - not much here
nmhau - nothing much how about you
nmhm - nothing much here, man
nmhu - nothing much here, you?
nmhwby - nothing much here what about you

nmjb - nothing much just bored
nmjc - not much, just chillin'
nmjch - Nothing Much Just Chilling
nmjcu - nothing much, just chilling, you?
nmjdhw - nothing much just doing homework
nmjfa - nothing much, just f**king around
nmnhnlm - no money, no honey, nobody loves me
nmp - Not My Problem
nmu - nothing much, you
nmw - no matter what
nmwh - no matter what happens
nn - good night
nn2r - no need to respond
nnaa - no not at all
nnfaa - no need for an apology
nnr - no not really
nntr - no need to reply
nntst - no need to say thanks
no pro - no problem
no1 - no one
noaa - National Oceanic and Atmospheric Administration
noc - naked on camera
noe - know
noes - no
nofi - No Flame Intended
nolm - No one loves me
nomw - not on my watch
noob - someone who is new
noobie - new person
nooblet - new player
noobz0r - newbie
noodz - nude pictures
nookie - sex
nop - normal operating procedure
norwich - knickers off ready when I come home
notin - nothing
noty - no thank you
noub - none of your business
nowai - No way
nowin - knowing

noyb - none of your business
noygdb - none of your god d**n business
np - no problem
np4np - naked pic for naked pic
npa - not paying attention
npc - Non-playable character
npe - nope
npgf - no problem girl friend
nph - no problem here
npi - no pun intended
npnt - no picture, no talk
nps - No Problems
nq - Thank you
nr - no reserve
nr4u - not right for you
nrg - energy
nrn - No Response Necessary
ns - nice
nsa - No Strings Attached
nsas - No Strings Attached Sex
nsfmf - not so fast my friend
nsfu - no sex for you
nsfw - not safe for work
nss - no s**t sherlock
nst - no school today
nstaafl - No Such Thing As a Free Lunch
nt - nice try
ntb - not to bad
ntbn - no text-back needed
nthg - nothing
nthin - nothing
nthn - nothing
ntigaf - not that i give a f**k
ntk - Need to know
ntkb - need to know basis
ntm - not to much
ntmk - Not to my knowledge
ntmu - nice to meet you
ntmy - nice to meet you
ntn - nothing

ntrly - Not Really
nts - note to self
ntstt - not safe to talk
ntt - need to talk
ntta - nothing to talk about
nttawwt - Not that there is anything wrong with that
nttiawwt - Not that there is anything wrong with that.
ntty - nice talking to you
ntw - not to worry
ntxt - no text
nty - no thank you
nu - new
nub - inexperienced person
nuff - enough
nuffin - nothing
nufin - nothing
nutin - nothing
nuttin - nothing
nv - envy
nvm - never mind
nvmd - nevermind
nvmdt - never mind then
nvmt - nevermind that
nvr - never
nvrm - Nevermind
nvrmnd - never mind
nw - no way
nwb - a new person
nwih - no way in hell
nwrus - no way are you serious
nws - not work safe
nwtf - now what the f**k
nwy - no way
nxt - next
ny1 - Anyone
nyc - New York City
nyf - not your fault
nyp - not your problem
nywy - anyway
o - Oh

o rly - oh really
o&o - over and out
o.p. - Original Poster
o/y - oh yeah
oaoa - over and over again
oar - on a roll
oaw - on a website
obgjfioyo - old but good job finding it on your own
obj - Object
obl - osama bin laden
obo - or best offer
obtw - oh, by the way
obv - obviously
obvi - obviously
occ - Occupation
ocd - obsessive compulsive disorder
ocgg - Oh Crap, gotta go
od - over dose
oday - software illegally obtained before it was released
odg - oh dear God
odtaa - one d**n thing after another
oe - or else
oed - oxford english dictionary
of10 - often
ofc - of course
ofcol - oh for crying out loud
ofn - Old f**king News
oftc - out for the count
oftn - often
oftpc - off topic
ofwg - old fat white guys
og - original gangster
ogw - oh guess what
oh noes - oh s**t!
oh noez - Oh no!
ohic - oh I see
ohn - oh hell no
ohnoez - Oh no
ohy - oh hell yeah
oibmpc - oops I broke my computer

oic - oh, I see
oicic - oh i see i see
oicu - oh, i see you!
oicwydt - oh, i see what you did there
oidia - oops i did it again
oiyd - Only In Your Dreams
oj - orange juice
ojsu - Oh, just shut up!
ok - okay
oll - online love
olpc - One Laptop Per Child
omdg - oh my dear god
omdz - Oh My Days
omfd - oh my f**king days
omfg - oh my f**king god
omfgn - Oh my f**king god noob
omfgsh - Oh My f**king Gosh
omfj - oh my f**king jesus
omfl - oh my f**king internet connection is slow
omfsm - Oh My Flying Spaghetti Monster
omfwtg - Oh My f**k What The God?
omg - oh my God
omg's - oh my god's
omgd - Oh my gosh dude
omgf - oh my god...f**k!
omgg - Oh my gosh girl
omgicfbi - Oh my god I can't f**king believe it
omgih - Oh My God In Heaven
omgihv2p - oh my god i have to pee
omginbd - Oh my God, It's no big deal
omgn - oh my goodness
omgny - oh my god no way
omgosh - Oh my gosh
omgroflmao - oh my god roll on the floor laughing my a** off
omgsh - oh my gosh
omgty - Oh my god thank you
omgukk - oh my god you killed kenny
omgwtf - on my God, what the f**k
omgwtfbbq - oh my God, what the f**k
omgwtfhax - Oh My God What The f**k, Hacks!

omgwtfit - Oh my God, what the f**k is that
omgwtfnipples - on my God, what the f**k
omgyg2bk - oh my god you got to be kidding
omgykkyb - oh my god you killed kenny you b*****ds
omgz - oh my God
omgzors - oh my god
omhg - oh my hell god
omj - oh my jesus
ommfg - oh my mother f**king god
omt - one more time
omw - on my way
omwh - on my way home
omwts - on my way to school
omy - oh my!
onoez - oh no
onoz - oh no
onud - oh no you didn't
onyd - oh no you didn't
oob - out of buisness
oobl - out of breath laughing
ooc - out of character
oohm - out of his/her mind
oom - Out of mana
oomf - One of my followers
oomm - out of my mind
ooo - out of the office
ootb - out of the blue
ootd - outfit of the day
oow - On our way
ooym - out of your mind
op - operator
orgy - orgasm
orlsx - oral sex
orly - Oh Really
orly - oh really?
orpg - online role playing game
os - operating system
osbutctt - only sad b*****ds use this crappy text talk
osd - On Screen Display
osifgt - oh s**t i forgot

oslt - or something like that
osy - oh screw you
ot - off topic
otc - off the chain
otfcu - on the floor cracking up
otfl - on the floor laughing
otflmao - On the floor laughing my a** off
otflmfao - On the floor laughing my f**king a** off
otflol - on the floor laughing out loud
otfp - on the f**king phone
otft - over the f**king top
oti - on the internet
otl - out to lunch
otoh - on the other hand
otp - on the phone
ots - over the shoulder
ott - over the top
otw - on the way
ova - over
oways - oh wow are you serious
owned - made to look bad
ownt - made to look bad
ownz - owns
ownzer - one who makes others look bad
ownzorz - Owned.
owt - Out
oww - Oops, wrong window
oyfe - Open Your f**king Eyes
oyid - oh yes i did
oyo - on your own
oyr - Oh Yeah Right
p-nis - penis
p.o.b. - Parent Over Back
p.o.s - parent over shoulder
p.o.s. - parent over shoulder
p/oed - pissed off
p/w - password
p00p - poop
p0wn - make to look bad
p2p - peer to peer

p33n - penis
p3n0r - penis
p3n15 - penis
p3n1s - penis
p4p - pic for pic
p911 - parent emergency (parent near)
p@w - parents are watching
pach - parents are coming home
pachs - parents are coming home soon
pae - Pimpin aint easy
pag - Parents Are Gone
pah - parents at home
parnts - parents
pas - parent at side
pasii - put a sock in it
patd - Panic At The Disco
paw - parents are watching
pb - peanut butter
pb&j - peanut butter and jelly
pbb - parent behind back
pbcakb - problem between chair and keyboard
pbj - peanut butter and jelly
pbjt - peanut butter jelly time
pbkc - Problem between keyboard & chair
pbly - probably
pbm - parent behind me
pbp - Please Be Patient
pcbd - page cannot be displayed
pce - peace
pcent - percent
pcm - please call me
pco - please come over
pcrs - Parents can read slang
pda - public display of affection
pdg - pretty d**n good
pdq - pretty d**n quick
peanus - penis
pearoast - repost
pebcak - Problem Exists Between Chair and Keyboard
pebkac - problem exists between keyboard and chair

pebmac - Problem Exist Between monitor and chair
peep dis - check out what I'm telling you
peeps - people
pen0r - Penis
pen15 - penis
penor - penis
peoples - people
perv - pervert
pewp - poop
pex - Please explain?
pezzas - parents
pf - profile
pfa - Please Find Attached
pfm - Please forgive me
pfo - please f**k off
pfos - parental figure over sholder
pfy - pimply faced youth
pg - page
ph# - phone number
ph33r - fear
ph34r - fear
phag - f**
phail - fail
phat - pretty hot and tasty
phayl - fail
phear - fear
phlr - peace hugs love respect
phm - please help me
phq - f**k you
phreak - freak
phreaker - phone hacker
phuck - f**k
phucker - f**ker
phuk - f**k
phun - fun
phux - f**k
phuxor - f**k
pic - picture
piccies - Pictures
pics - pictures

pihb - pee in his/her butt
piihb - put it in her butt
piitb - put it in the butt
pima - Pain in my a**
pimfa - pain in my f**king a**
pimha - Pain in my hairy a**
pimpl - pissing in my pants laughing
pino - Filipino
pir - parents in room
pirlos - parent in room looking over shoulder
pita - pain in the a**
pitfa - Pain In The f**king a**
pitr - parent in the room
pitrtul - parents in the room text you later
piw - Parent is watching
pix - pictures
pk - player kill
pkemon - pokemon
pker - player killer
pking - player killing
pl - parent looking
pl0x - please
pl8 - plate
plac - parent looking at computer
plams - parents looking at my screen
plars - party like a rock star
platcs - parent looking at the computer screen
ple's - please
pleaz - please
pleez - please
pleeze - please
pleze - please
pliz - please
plma - please leave me alone
plmk - please let me know
plocks - please
plom - parents looking over me
plomb - parents looking over my back
ploms - parent looking over my shoulder
plos - Parents Looking Over Shoulder

plox - please
ploxxorz - please
pls - please
plse - please
plx - please/thanks
plywm - play with me
plz - please
plzkthx - Please? OK, Thank you
plzthx - please? Thanks
pmfji - Pardon me for jumping in
pmfsl - piss my f**king self laughing
pmg - oh my God
pmita - pound me in the a**
pmitap - pound me in the a** prison
pml - pissing myself laughing
pmo - pissing me off
pmp - pissing my pants
pmpl - piss my pants laughing
pmsfl - Pissed Myself f**king Laughing
pmsl - piss my self laughing
pnbf - Potential new boy friend
pnhlgd - parents not home, let's get dirty
pns - penis
pnus - penis
po - piss off
po po - police
po'd - pissed off
pob - parent over back
poc - Piece of crap
poed - pissed off
poets - piss off early, tomorrow's Saturday
poi - point of interest
poidnh - Pics or it did not happen
pol - parent over looking
poms - parent over my shoulder
poo - poop
poontang - female genitalia
pooter - Computer
popo - police
poq - Piss Off Quick

pos - Parent Over Shoulder
poscs - parents over sholder change subject
posmbri - parent over shoulder might be reading it
potc - pirates of the caribbean
pots - Plain Old Telephone Service
pov - point of view
pow - prisoner of war
pp - pee pee
ppl - people
ppls - people
pplz - people
ppor - post proof or recant
ppppppp - Prior Proper Planning Prevents Piss Poor Performance
pr0 - professional
pr0n - porn
pr0nz - porn
prblm - Problem
prd - period
preggers - pregnant
prego - Pregnant
prfct - perfect
prn - porn
prncpl - principal
prncss - princess
prnoscrn - porn on screen
pro - professional
prob - problem
probly - probably
probz - probably
prod - product
prolly - Probably
prollz - probably
pron - porn
proxie - proxy
prp - please reply
prsn - person
prty - party
prv - private
prvrt - pervert
prw - parents are watching

ps1 - Play Station 1
ps2 - Play Station 2
ps3 - Play Station 3
psa - Public Service Announcement
psbms - parent standing by my side
psn - playstation netwok
psos - parent standing over sholder
psp - playstation portable
pssy - p***y
pst - please send tell
pt33n - preteen
ptbb - pa** the barf bag
ptfo - passed the f**k out
pthc - preteen hardcore
ptl - Praise the Lord
pto - Personal Time Off
ptw - play to win
puh-leaze - Please
purty - pretty
puter - Computer
pvp - player versus player
pvt - pervert
pw - parent watching
pwb - p***y whipped b***h
pwcb - parents watching close by
pwd - password
pwn - made to look bad
pwn3d - owned
pwn3r - owner
pwnage - Ownage
pwnd - owned
pwned - made to look bad
pwner - owner
pwnt - owned
pwnz - owns
pwnzor - owner
pwob - Parent watching over back
pwoms - parent watching over my shoulder
pwor - power
pwos - parent was over sholder

pww - parents were watching
pxr - punk rocker
pydim - put your d**k in me
pyfco - put your freaking clothes on
pyt - pretty young thing
pz - peace
pzled - puzzled
p^s - parent over shoulder
q2c - quick to c**
q33r - Queer
q4u - question for you
qed - I've made my Point
qfe - quoted for emphasis
qfmft - quoted for motherf**king truth
qft - quoted for truth
qft&gj - quoted for truth and great justice
ql - cool
qltm - quietly laughing to myself
qna - question and answer
qool - cool
qoolz - cool
qotd - quote of the day
qotsa - queens of the stone age
qoty - quote of the year
qpr - quite pathetic really
qpwd - quit posting while drunk
qq - crying eyes
qt - cutie
qt3.14 - cutie pie
qte - cutie
qtpi - cutie pie
r - are
r-tard - retard
r.i.p. - rest in peace
r0x0rz - rocks
r2f - Ready To f**k
r8 - rate
r8p - rape
r8pist - rapist
r8t - rate

ra2 - red alert 2 (game)
ra3 - Red Alert 3 (game)
raoflmao - rolling around on floor laughing my a** off
rawk - Rock
rawks - rocks
rawr - roar
rb@u - right back at you
rbau - right back at you
rbay - right back at you
rbm - right behind me
rbtl - Read between the lines
rbty - right back to you
rcks - Rocks
rcsa - right click save as
rcvd - received
rdy - ready
re - reply
re/rehi - hello again
reefer - marijuana
refl - rolling on the floor laughing
rehi - hello again
rele - really
rents - parents
rentz - parents
rep - to represent
reppin - representing
retrotextual - One who is using out of date words and abbreviations while texting.
rff - really f**king funny
rflmao - rolling on the floor laughing my a** off
rfn - right f**king now
rgr - roger
rhcp - red hot chilli peppers
rhgir - really hot guy in room
rhs - right hand side
ricl - rolling in chair laughing
rifk - rolling on the floor laughing
rihad - Rot In Hell And Die
rino - republican in name only
rite - right

ritjive - non virgin
rjct - reject
rl - real life
rlbf - Real Life Boy Friend
rlf - Real Life Friend
rlg - really loud giggle
rlgf - Real Life Girl Friend
rlly - really
rln - real life name
rly - really
rlz - rules
rlze - realize
rm - room
rme - rolling my eyes
rmr - remember
rmso - Rock My socks off
rn - Right now
rnt - aren't
ro - rock out
rockr - rocker
rodger - affirmative
rofalol - roll on the floor and laugh out loud
rofc - Rolling On Floor Crying
roffle - rolling on the floor laughing
roffle out loud - rolling on the floor laughing out loud
rofflecake - rolling on the floor laughing
rofflecopters - rolling on the floor with laughter
roffleol - rolling on the floor laughing out loud
roffles - rolling on floor laughing
rofflmfao - rolling on the floor laughing my f**king a**
rofl - rolling on the floor laughing
rofl&pmp - rolling on floor laughing and peeing my pants
roflao - rolling on the floor laughing my a** off
roflastc - Rolling On Floor Laughing And Scaring The Cat
roflcopter - Rolling on the floor laughing
roflcopters - rolling on the floor laughing, VERY funny.
roflkmd - rolling on the floor laughing kicking my dog
rofllh - rolling on the floor laughing like hell
roflmao - rolling on the floor laughing my a** off
roflmaoapimp - rolling on the floor laughing my a** off and

peeing in my pants
roflmaool - Rolling on the floor laughing my a** off out loud
roflmaopmp - rolling on the floor, laughing my a** off, pissing my pants
roflmaouts - Rolling on floor laughing my f**king a** off unable to speak
roflmaowpimp - rolling on floor laughing my a** off while peeing in my pants
roflmbfao - Rolling On Floor Laughing My Big Fat a** Off
roflmbo - rolling on floor laughing my butt off
roflmfaopimp - rolling on the floor laughing my f**king a** off pissing in my pants
roflmfaopmp - rolling on flor laughing my f**king a** of peeing my pants
roflmgao - rolling on the floor laughing my gay a** off
roflmgdao - rolling on the floor laughing my god d**n a** off
roflmgdmfao - roling on floor laughing my god d**n mother f**king a** off
roflmgo - Rolling On Floor Laughing My Guts Out
roflmho - Rolling on the floor laughing my head off
roflmiaha - Rolling on the floor laughing myself into a heart attack
roflmmfao - rolling on the floor laughing my mother f**king a** off
roflol - rolling on floor laughing out loud
roflolbag - Rolling On The Floor Laughing Out Loud Busting A Gut
roflpimp - rolling on the floor laughing pissing in my pants
roflpmp - rolling on the floor laughing peeing my pants
roflwtime - Rolling on the Floor laughing with tears in my eyes
rofpml - rolling on the floor pissing myself laughing
rofwl - Rolling on the floor while laughing
roger - affirmative
rogl - rolling on ground laughing
roglmfao - rolling on ground laughing my f**king a** off
roi - Return On Investment
roids - steroids
roj - affirmative
rol - rolling over laugihng
rolmao - Rolling Over Laughing My a** Off

rolmfao - rolling over laughing my f**king a** off
rombl - rolled off my bed laughing
rong - wrong
roofles - rolling on the floor laughing
ror - raughing out roud
rotf - rolling on the floor
rotfalol - roll on the floor and laugh out loud
rotffl - roll on the f**king floor laughing
rotfflmao - rolling on the f**king floor laughing my a** off
rotfflmfao - rolling on the f**king floor laughing my f**king a** off
rotfl - rolling on the floor laughing
rotflaviab - rolling on the floor laughing and vomiting in a bucket
rotflmao - rolling on the floor laughing my a** off
rotflmaofaktd - Rolling on the floor laughing my a** off farted and killed the dog
rotflmaool - rolling on the floor laughing my a** off out loud
rotflmaostc - rolling on the floor laughing my a** off scaring the cat
rotflmbo - rolling on the floor laughing my butt off
rotflmfao - rolling on the floor laughing my f**king a** off
rotflmfaopimp - rolling on the floor laughing my f**king a** off peeing
in my pants
rotflmfaopmp - rolling on the floor laughing my a** off pissin my pants
rotflmfho - rolling on the floor laughing my f**king head off
rotflmho - rolling on the floor laughing my head off
rotflmmfao - rolling on the floor laughing my mother f**king a** off
rotflol - rolling on the floor laughing out loud
rotfpm - rolling on the floor pissing myself
rotfwlmao - rolling on the floor while laughing my a** off
rotg - rolling on the ground
rotgl - roll on the ground laughing
rotglmao - rolling on the ground laughing my a** off
rotw - rest of the world
rowyco - rock out with your c**k out
rox - rocks
roxor - rock
roxorz - rocks

roxxor - rock
rp - roleplay
rpg - role playing game
rpita - royal pain in the a**
rplbk - reply back
rpo - royally pissed off
rq - real quick
rr - rest room
rrb - restroom break
rsn - real soon now
rsp - respawn
rspct - respect
rsps - Runescape Private Server
rta - read the article
rtard - retard
rtbq - Read The Blinking Question
rtf - return the favor
rtfa - read the f**king article
rtffp - Read the f**king front page
rtfm - read the f**king manual
rtfmfm - read the f**king manual f**king moron
rtfmm - read the f**king manual moron
rtfms - Read The f**king Manual Stupid
rtfp - read the f**king post
rtfq - Read The f**king Question
rtfs - read the f**king summary
rtfu - Ready the f**k up
rtg - ready to go
rtl - report the loss
rtm - read the manual
rtr - Read the Rules
rtry - retry
rts - Real-time strategy
ru - are you
ru18 - are you 18
rua - are you alone
ruabog - are you a boy or girl
ruagoab - are you a girl or a boy
rubz2nt - are you busy tonight
rufkm - are you f**king kidding me

rugay - are you gay
rugta - are you going to answer
ruh - are you horny
ruk - are you ok?
rukm - are you kidding me
rumf - Are you male or female
ruok - are you ok?
rur - are you ready
rut - are you there
ruwm - are you watching me
rwb - Rich White b***h
ryt - right
ryte - right
s - smile
s'ok - it's okay
s'pose - suppose
s'up - what is up
s.i.n.g.l.e - Stay intoxicated nightly, get laid everyday.
s.i.t. - stay in touch
s.o.a.b. - son of a b***h
s.o.b. - son of a b***h
s.w.a.k. - sealed with a kiss
s/b - should be
s2a - sent to all
s2bu - Sucks to be you
s2r - send to receive
s2u - same to you
s2us - Speak to you soon
s3x - Sex.
s4se - Sight For Sore Eyes
s8ter - skater
sab - slap a b***h
sagn - Spelling and Grammar Nazi
sah - sexy as hell
sahm - stay at home mom
sase - self addressed stamped envelope
sbc - sorry bout caps
sbcg4ap - strongbads cool game for attractive people
sbd - silent but deadly
sblai - stop babbaling like an idiot

sbrd - so bored
sbs - such bull s**t
sbt - sorry bout that
scnr - sorry, I couldn't resist
scool - school
scrilla - money
scrt - secret
scurred - scared
sd - suck d**k
sdf^ - shut da f**k up
sdk - Software Development Kit
sdlc - Software Development Life Cycle
sec - second
secks - sex
secksea - Sexy
secksy - sexy
sed - said
see through your eyes - stye
seg - s**t Eatin Grin
seks - sex
sellin - selling
seo - Search Engine Optimization
serp - search engine results page
sexc - sexy
sexe - sexy
sexi - Sexy
sexii - sexy
sexilicious - Very Sexy
sexx0rz - sex
sez - says
sfam - Sister from another mother
sfe - safe
sfh - So f**king Hot
sfipmp - so funny I peed my pants
sfm - so f**king much
sfr - so f**king random
sfs - so f**king stupid
sfsg - So far so good
sfu - shut the f**k up
sfw - safe for work

sfwuz - safe for work until zoomed
sfy - speak for yourself
sg - so good
sgb - straight/gay/bisexual
sgbadq - Search google before asking dumb questions
sgi - Still got it
sgtm - slightly gigling to myself
sh - s**t happens
shag - f**k
shawty - girl
shd - should
shexi - sexy
shexy - sexy
shiat - s**t
shiet - s**t
shite - s**t
shiz - s**t
shizit - s**t
shiznat - s**t
shiznit - s**t
shizz - s**t
shizzle - s**t
shld - should
shmexy - sexy
shmily - see how much i love you
sho - sure
sho'nuff - sure enough
showin - showing
shrn - so hot right now
sht - s**t
shtf - s**t hits the fan
shud - should
shuddup - Shut Up
shup - shut up
shure - sure
shut^ - shut Up
shwr - shower
shyat - s**t
shyt - s**t
siao - school is almost over

sibir - sibling in room
sic - said in context
sicl - sitting in chair laughing
sif - as if
sifn't - as if not
sig - Signature
siggy - Signature
silf - Sister I'd Like To f**k
simcl - sitting in my chair laughing
simclmao - sitting in my chair laughing my a** off
siol - Shout It Out Loud
sis - sister
sista - Sister
sitb - sex in the but
sitmf - say it to my face
siu - suck it up
siuya - shove it up your a**
sk - spawn kill
sk8 - skate
sk8er - skater
sk8ing - Skating
sk8r - skater
sk8ter - skater
sk8tr - skater
sked - schedule
skeet - ejaculate
skewl - school
skhool - school
skillz - skills
skl - School
skool - school
skoul - school
sktr - skater
skwl - school
sl4n - so long for now
sleepin - sleeping
sleepn - sleeping
slf - sexy little f**k
slgb - Straight/Lesbian/Gay/Bisexual
slng - slang

slo - slow
slore - s**tty w***e
slos - someone looking over shoulder
slp - sleep
slt - something like that
sl^t - s**t
sm - social media
sm1 - someone
smb - see my blog
smbd - suck my big d**k
smbt - Suck my big toe
smc - suck my c**k
smd - suck my d**k
smdb - suck my d**k b***h
smdvq - suck my d**k quickly
smeg - f**k
smexy - sexy
smf - stupid motherf**ker
smfd - suck my f**king d**k
smfpos - stupid mother f**king piece of s**t
smh - shaking my head
smhb - suck my hairy balls
smho - Screaming My Head Off
smithwaws - Smack me in the head with a wooden spoon
smofo - stupid mother f**ker
smst - somebody missed snack time
smt - suck my tits
smthin - something
smthng - something
smtm - sometime
smto - Sticking My Tongue Out
smtoay - Sticking my tongue out at you
sn - screen name
snafu - situation normal all f**ked up
snafubar - Situation Normal All f**ked Up Beyond Any Recognition
snes - Super Nintendo Entertainment System
snew - what's new
snf - so not fair
snl - Saturday Night Live

snm - say no more
snog - kiss
snogged - kissed
soa - service oriented architecture
soab - son of a btch
soad - system of a down
soafb - son of a f**king b***h
sob - son of a b***h
sobs - same, old, boring s**t
soc - Same old crap
soe - service oriented enterprise
sof - smile on face
sofas - stepping out for a smoke
sofs - same old f**king s**t
soi - service oriented infrastructure
sok - It's ok
sokay - it's okay
sol - s**t outta luck
som'm - something
som1 - someone
somadn - sitting on my a** doing nothing
some1 - someone
soml - story of my life
soo - So
soobs - saggy boobs
sool - s**t out of luck
sop - same old place
sorg - Straight or Gay
sorreh - sorry
sorta - sort of
sos - same old s**t
sosdd - same old s**t, different day
sosg - spouse over shoulder gone
sot - suck on this
sotc - stupid off topic crap
sotr - sex on the road
sowi - sorry
sowwy - sorry
soz - sorry
spk - speak

sploits - exploits
sploitz - exploits
spos - stupid peace of s**t
sprm - sperm
sqtm - snickering quietly to myself
srch - search
srly - seriously
sroucks - that's cool, but it still sucks
srry - sorry
srs - serious
srsly - seriously
srvis - Service
sry - sorry
srynd2g - sorry need to go
srzly - seriously
ss - screenshot
ss4l - smoking sista for life
ssdd - same s**t, different day
ssdp - same s**t different pile
ssia - subject says it all
ssl - secure sockets layer
ssob - stupid sons of b***hes
ssry - so sorry
sssd - Same s**t Same Day
st - Stop That
st1 - stoned
st8 - state
stb - soon to be
stbx - soon to be ex
stby - sucks to be you
std - sexually transmitted disease
steamloller - Laughing. Alot.
stfd - sit the f**k down
stff - stuff
stfm - search the f**king manual
stfng - search the f**king news group
stfu - shut the f**k up
stfua - shut the f**k up already
stfuah - shut the f**k up a**h**e
stfub - shut the f**k up b***h

stfuda - Shut the f**k up dumb a**
stfugbtw - shut the f**k up and get back to work
stfun - Shut the f**k up n****r
stfuogtfo - Shut the f**k up or get the f**k out.
stfuppercut - shut the f**k up
stfuyb - shut the f**k up you b***h
stfuysoab - shut the f**k up you son of a b***h
stfw - search the f**king web
stg - swear to god
sth - something
sthing - something
sthu - shut the hell up
stm - smiling to myself
stoopid - stupid
stpd - stupid
str8 - straight
str8up - straight up
sts - so to speak
stsp - Same Time Same Place
stt - Same time tomorrow
stufu - stupid f**ker
stupd - stupid
stw - share the wealth
stys - speak to you soon
su - shut up
suabq - shut up and be quiet
suagooml - shut up and get out of my life
suib - shut up im busy
suk - suck
suka - Sucker
sukz - sucks
sul - see you later
sum1 - someone
sumfin - Something
summin - something
sumone - someone
sumthin' - Something
sumtin - something
sup - what's up
supa - super

supposably - Supposedly
sus - see you soon
susfu - situation unchanged, still f**ked up
sut - see you tomorrow
sutuct - so you think you can type
sux - sucks
sux0rz - sucks
sux2bu - sucks to be you
suxor - Sucks
suxors - sucks
suxorz - sucks
suxx - sucks
suxxor - sucks
suyah - shut up you a** hole!
svn - seven
svu - special victims unit
sw - so what
swafk - sealed with a friendly kiss
swak - sealed with a kiss
swakaah - Sealed With A Kiss And A Hug
swalk - sealed with a loving kiss
swf - single white female
swm - single white male
swmbo - she who must be obeyed
swmt - Stop Wasting My Time
swp - sorry wrong person
swsw2b - single when she wants to be
swt - sweet
swtf - seriously, what the f**k
sx - sex
sxc - sexy
sxcy - sexy
sxe - straight edge
sxi - sexy
sxs - sex
sxy - sexy
syatp - see you at the party
sydim - stick your d**k in me
sydlm - Shut your dirty little mouth
syfm - shut your f**king mouth

syiab - see you in a bit
syiaf - see you in a few
syl - see you later
syl8r - see you later
sym - shut your mouth
syoa - Save Your Own a**
syotbf - see you on the battlefield
syrs - see ya real soon
sys - see you soon
sysop - system operator
syt - see you there
sytycd - so you think you can dance
syu - sex you up
sz - sorry
t#3 - the
t,ftfy - there, fixed that for you
t.t.y.l - Talk To You Later
t/a - Try again
t2b - time to blunt
t2m - talk to me
t2u - talking to you
t2ul - talk to you later
t2ul8r - talk to you later
t3h - the
t4a - thanks for asking
t4m - Transgender for Male
t8st - taste
ta - thanks again
taci - that's a crappy idea
tafn - That's all for now
taht - that
tai - think about it
taig - That's all I got.
tal - thanks a lot
tanq - thank you
tanstaafl - there ain't no such thing as a free lunch
tard - retard
tarfu - things are really f**ked up
tat - that
tat2 - tattoo

tau - thinking about you
taunch - te amo un chingo
taw - Teachers are Watching
tay - thinking about you
tb - text back
tb4u - too bad for you
tba - to be anounced
tbc - To be continued
tbd - to be decided
tbf - to be fair
tbfh - to be f**king honest
tbfu - too bad for you
tbh - to be honest
tbhimo - to be honest in my opinion
tbnt - thanks but no thanks
tbp - The Pirate Bay
tbpfh - To be perfectly f**king honest
tbph - To be perfectly honest
tbqf - to be quite frank
tbqh - to be quite honest
tbss - too bad so sad
tbtfh - to be totally freaking honest
tbvh - to be very honest
tc - take care
tcfc - Too Close For Comfort
tcfm - too cool for me
tcg - Trading Card Game
tchbo - Topic creater has been owned
tcial - The cake is a lie
tcoy - take care of yourself
tcp - transmission control protocol
tcp/ip - transmission control protocol/internet protocol
td2m - talk dirty to me
tddup - till death do us part
tdf - To Die For
tdl - Too d**n Lazy
tdtm - Talk Dirty To Me
tdwdtg - The Devil Went Down To Georgia
te - Team effort
teh - the

teotwawki - the end of the world as we know it
terd - s**t
tf2 - Team Fortress 2
tfa - the f**king article
tfb - time for bed
tfbundy - totaly f**ked but unfortunatly not dead yet
tfc - Team Fortress Classic
tfd - total f**king disaster
tff - That's f**king Funny
tfft - thank f**k for that
tffw - Too funny for words
tfh - Thread from hell
tfic - Tongue Firmly In Cheek
tfiik - the f**k if i know
tfl - Thanks For Looking
tfln - thanx for last night
tfm - too f**king much
tfs - thanks for sharing
tfta - thanks for the add
tfti - thanks for the information
tfu - that's f**ked up
tfu2baw - time for you to buy a watch
tg - thank god
tgfe - together forever
tgfitw - The Greatest Fans In The World
tgft - thank god for that
tgfu - too good for you
tgfuap - thank god for unanswered prayers
tghig - thank god husband is gone
tgif - thank god it's friday
tgiff - thank god its f**king Friday
tgis - thank god it's saturday
tgiwjo - Thank God It Was Just Once
tgsttttptct - thank God someone took the time to put this crap together
tgtbt - Too Good To Be True
tgwig - thank god wife is gone
tgws - that goes without saying
th@ - that
tha - the

thankies - Thank You
thankx - thank you
thanq - thank you
thanx - thank you
thar - there
thatz - that's
thku - thank you
thn - then
thnk - think
thnx - thanks
tho - though
thot - the hoe of today
thr - there
thr4 - therefore
thru - through
tht - that
thwdi - thats how we do it
thwy - the hell with you!
thx - thank you
thxx - thanks
thz - thank you
ti2o - that is too obious
tia - thanks in advance
tiafayh - Thanks in advance for all your help
tiai - take it all in
tias - Try It And See
tiatwtcc - this is a trap word to catch copiers
tif - this is fun
tif2m - this is f**king 2 much
tifs - this is funny s**t
tifu - that is f**ked up
tigger - tiger
tiic - the idiots in control
til - until
tilf - Teenager I'd Like To f**k
tinf - this is not fair
tinla - this is not legal advice
tinstaafl - There Is No Such Thing As A Free Lunch
tioli - take it or leave it
tis - is

tisc - that is so cool
tisfu - that is so f**ked up
tisg - this is so gay
tisly - that is so last year
tisnf - that is so not fair
tiss - This is some s**t
tisw - that is so wrong
tiw - teacher is watching
tix - tickets
tjb - thats just boring
tk - team kill
tk2ul - talk to you later
tkd - Tae Kwon Do
tker - team killer
tks - thanks
tku - thank you
tl - Tough Luck
tl,dr - Too long; didn't read
tl8r - talk later
tl:dr - Too Long; Didn't Read
tl; dr - To Long; Didn't read
tl;dr - too long; didn't read
tla - Three Letter Acronym
tlc - tender loving care
tld - told
tldnr - too long, did not read
tldr - Too long, didn't read.
tlgo - The list goes on
tliwwv - this link is worthless without video
tlk - talk
tlk2me - talk to me
tlk2ul8r - talk to you later
tlkin - talking
tlkn - talking
tltpr - Too long to proof read.
tlyk - to let you know
tma - take my advice
tmaai - tell me all about it
tmai - tell me about it
tmbi - tell me about it

tmi - too much information
tmk - to my knowledge
tml - tell me later
tmmrw - tomorrow
tmnt - teenage mutant ninja turtles
tmo - take me out
tmoro - tomorrow
tmoz - tomorrow
tmr - tomorrow
tmr@ia - the monkeys are at it again
tmrrw - tomorrow
tmrw - Tomorrow
tmrz - tomorrow
tms - that makes sense
tmsaisti - That's my story and I'm sticking to it.
tmsg - tell me something good
tmsidk - tell me somthing I don't know
tmth - too much to handle
tmtmo - text me tomorrow
tmtoyh - Too Much Time On Your Hands
tmtt - tell me the truth
tmw - Too much work
tmwfi - Take my word for it
tmz - tomorrow
tn1 - trust no-one
tna - tits and a**
tnf - That's Not Funny
tnlnsl - Took nothing left nothing signed log
tnx - thanks
tnxz - thanks
tob - teacher over back
tofy - Thinking of You
toh - typing one handed
tok - That's ok
tok2ul8r - i'll talk to you later
tolol - thinking of laughing out loud
tomm - tommorow
tomoz - tomorrow
tos - terms of service
totl - total

totm - top of the morning
totp - talking on the phone
totpd - top of the page dance
tou - thinking of you
toya - thinking of you always
tp - toilet paper
tpb - the pirate bay
tpiwwp - this post is worthless without pictures
tps - test procedure specification
tptb - the powers that be
tq - Thank You
trani - transexual
tranny - Transexual
trble - trouble
trd - tired
trnsl8 - translate
trnsltr - translator
troll - person who diliberately stirs up trouble
tru - true
ts - talking s**t
tsc - that's so cool
tsff - thats so f**kin funny
tsig - that site is gay
tsnf - that's so not fair
tss - That's so sweet
tstoac - too stupid to own a computer
tswc - tell someone who cares
tt4n - ta ta for now
ttbc - Try to be cool
ttbomk - to the best o fmy knowledge
ttc - text the cell
ttfaf - Through the Fire and Flames
ttfn - ta ta for now
tthb - try to hurry back
ttihlic - try to imagine how little i care
ttiuwiop - this thread is useless without pics
ttiuwop - this thread is useless without pics
ttiuwp - This Thread Is Useless Without Pictures
ttiwwop - This thread is worthless without pics
ttiwwp - this thread is worthless without pics

ttl - total
ttlly - totally
ttly - totally
ttm - talk to me
ttml - talk to me later
ttms - talking to myself
ttr - time to run
ttrf - That's the rules, f**ker
tts - text to speech
ttt - to the top
ttth - Talk To The Hand
tttt - to tell the truth
ttul - Talk To You Later
ttul8r - Talk to you later
ttus - talk to you soon
ttut - Talk to you Tomorrow
ttutt - to tell you the truth
tty - Talk to You
ttyab - Talk to you after breakfast
ttyad - Talk to you after Dinner
ttyal - Talk to you after lunch
ttyas - talk to you at school
ttyiam - talk to you in a minute
ttyitm - talk to you in the morning
ttyl - talk to you later
ttyl8r - talk to you later
ttylo - talk to you later on
ttylt - talk to you later today
ttyn - talk to you never
ttyna - talk to you never again
ttynl - talk to you never loser
ttynw - talk to you next week
ttyo - talk to you online
ttyotp - talk to you on the phone
ttyrs - talk to you really soon
ttys - talk to you soon
ttyt - talk to you tomorrow
ttytm - talk to you tomorrow
ttytt - to tell you the truth
ttyw - talk to you whenever

ttywl - Talk to you way later
tu - thank you
tuff - tough
tuh - to
tut - take your time
tuvm - thank you very much
tv - television
tvm - thanks very much
tw - Teacher Watching
twajs - That was a joke, son.
twat - vagina
twbc - that would be cool
twdah - that was dumb as hell
twf - That was funny
twfaf - thats what friends are for
twg - That was great
twi - Texting While Intoxicated
twis - that's what I said
twoh - typing with one hand
tws2wa - That was so 2 weeks ago
twss - That's what she said
twsy - That was so yeterday
twttr - twitter
twvsoy - that was very stupid of you
twyl - Talk With You Later
twys - Talk With You Soon
tx - thanks
txs - thanks
txt - text
txting - texting
txtyl - text you later
ty - thank you
tyclos - turn your CAPS LOCK off, stupid
tyfi - Thank You for invite
tyfn - thank you for nothing
tyfyc - Thank You For Your Comment
tyfyt - Thank you for your time
tyl - text you later
tym - time
tyme - time

typ - thank you partner
typo - typing mistake
tyred - tired
tys - Told You So
tysfm - thank you so f**king much
tysm - thank you so much
tysvm - thank you so very much
tyt - take your time
tyto - take your top off
tyty - thank you thank you
tyvm - Thank You Very Much
tyvvm - thank you very very much
u - you
u iz a 304 - you is a hoe
u'd - you would
u'll - you will
u'r - you're
u'v - you have
u've - You've
u/l - upload
u/n - username
u2 - You too
u2u - up to you
u4i - up for it
ua - user agreement
uaaaa - Universal Association Against Acronym Abuse
uat - User Acceptance Testing
uayor - Use At Your Own Risk
ub3r - super
uber - over
uctaodnt - you can't teach an old dog new tricks
udc - you don't care
udek - you don't even know
uds - you dumb s**t
udwk - you don't want to know
udy - you done yet
ufab - ugly fat a** b***h
ufia - unsolicited finger in the anus
ufic - Unsolicited Finger in Chili
ufmf - you funny mother f**ker

ugba - you gay b***h a**
ugtr - you got that right
uhab - you have a blog
uhems - you hardly ever make sense
ui - User Interface
ujds - u just did s**t
ukr - You know right
ukwim - you know what i mean
ul - unlucky
ulbom - you looked better on myspace
umfriend - sexual partner
un2bo - you need to back off
un4rtun8ly - unfortunately
unt - until next time
uom - You owe me
upcia - unsolicited pool cue in anus
upia - unsolicited pencil in anus
upmo - You piss me off
upos - you piece of s**t
upw - unidentified party wound
ur - your
ur2g - you are too good
ur6c - you're sexy
ura - you are a
uradrk - you're a dork
urafb - you are a f**king b***h
uraqt - you are a cutie
urcrzy - you are crazy
ure - you are
urg - you are gay
urht - you're hot
url8 - you are late
urms - you rock my socks
urmw - you are my world
urnc - you are not cool
urs - yours
ursab - you are such a b***h
ursdf - you are so d**n fine
ursg - you are so gay
ursh - you are so hot

urssb - you are so sexy baby
urstpid - you are stupid
urstu - you are stupid
urtb - you are the best
urtbitw - You are the best in the world!
urtrd - you retard
urtw - you are the worst
urw - you are weird
uryyfm - you are too wise for me
usck - you suck
usd - United States Dollar
ussr - The Union of Soviet Socialist Republics
usuk - You Suck
usux - you suck
ut - unreal tournament
ut - you there
utfs - Use the f**king search
utfse - use the f**king search engine
utm - you tell me
uttm - you talking to me?
utube - youtube
utw - used to work
uty - it's up to you
uve - You've
uvgtbsm - you have got to be shiting me
uw - you're welcome
uwc - you are welcome
uya - up your a**
uyab - up your a** b***h
v4g1n4 - vagina
vag - vagina
vajayjay - vagina
vb - visual basic
vbeg - very big evil grin
vbg - very big grin
vf - very funny
vfe - Virgins 4 ever
vff - Verry f**king Funny
vfm - value for money
vgg - very good game

vgh - Very good hand
vgl - very good looking
vid - Video
vids - Videos
vip - very important person
vleo - Very Low Earth Orbit
vlog - video log
vn - very nice
vnc - Virtual Network Computing
vnh - Very nice hand
voip - voice over ip
vrsty - Varsity
vry - very
vwd - very well done
vweg - very wicked evil grin
vzit - visit
vzn - verizon
w'sup - what's up
w.b.s. - Write Back Soon
w.e - Whatever
w.e. - whatever
w.o.w - World of Warcraft
w.o.w. - world of warcraft
w/ - with
w/b - write back
w/e - whatever
w/end - weekend
w/eva - whatever
w/o - with out
w/out - without
w/u - with you
w00t - woohoo
w012d - word
w2d - what to do
w2f - want to f**k
w2g - Way to go
w2ho - want to hang out
w2m - want to meet
w33d - weed
w8 - wait

w8am - wait a minute
w8ing - waiting
w8t4me - wait for me
w8ter - waiter
w911 - Wife in room
wab - what a b***h
wad - without a doubt
wad ^ - what's up?
wadr - with all due respect
wadzup - What's up?
waf - weird as f**k
wafda - What a f**king Dumb a**
wafl - what a f**king loser
wafm - wait a f**king minute
wafn - what a f**ken noob
wai - what an idiot
waloc - what a load of crap
walstib - what a long strange trip it's been
wam - wait a minute
wamh - with all my heart
wan2tlk - Want to talk
wana - want to
wanafuk - wanna f**k
wanker - masturbater
wanking - Masturbating
wanna - want to
wansta - wanna be ganster
warez - illegally obtained software
wassup - what's up?
wasup - What's Up
was^ - What's Up
wat - what
wat's^ - Whats Up
watcha - what are you
watev - whatever
wateva - whatever
watevr - whatever
watevs - whatever
wats - whats
wats ^ - whats up

wats^ - what's up?
watz ^ - What's up
wau - what about you
waug - Where are you going
wauw - what are you wearing
wau^2 - what are you up to?
waw - what a w***e
waycb - when are you coming back
wayd - what are you doing
waygow - who are you going out with
wayh - why are you here
wayn - Where Are You Now
waysttm - why are you still talking to me
waysw - Why are you so weird
wayt - What are you thinking?
wayta - what are you talking about
wayut - what are you up to
waz - what is
waz ^ - what's up
wazz - what's
wazza - what's up
wazzup - what's up
waz^ - what's up?
wb - welcome back
wbagnfarb - would be a good name for a rock band
wbb - will be back
wbbs - will be back soon
wbp - Welcome Back Partner
wbrb - Will be right back
wbs - write back soon
wbu - what about you
wby - what about you
wc - who cares
wc3 - Warcraft III
wcutm - what can you tell me
wcw - webcam w***e
wd - well done
wdf - Worth Dying For
wdhlm - why doesnt he love me?
wdidn - what do i do now

wdim - What Did I miss
wdtm - what does that mean
wduc - what do you care
wdum - what do you mean
wdus - What Did You Say
wdut - what do you think?
wdutom - what do you think of me
wduw - what do you want
wduwta - what do you wanna talk about
wduwtta - what do you want to talk about
wdwdn - what do we do now
wdwgw - where did we go wrong
wdydt - why do you do that
wdye - What do you expect
wdyl - who do you like
wdym - what do you mean
wdys - What did you say
wdyt - what do you think
wdytia - who do you think i am?
wdyw - what do you want
wdywd - what do you want to do?
wdywtd - what do you want to do
wdywtdt - Why Do You Want To Do That?
wdywtta - what do you want to talk about
webby - webcam
weg - wicked evil grin
welc - welcome
wen - when
werkz - works
wev - Whatever
weve - what ever
wevr - whatever
wfh - Working From Home
wfhw - what's for homework
wfm - Works For Me
wfyb - whatever floats your boat
wg - wicked gril
wgac - who gives a crap
wgaf - Who gives a f**k
wgas - who gives a s**t

wgasa - who gives a s**t anyway
wgo - what's going on
wgph2 - Want to go play Halo 2?
wha - what?
whaddya - what do you
whaletail - thong
whatcha - what are you
whatev - whatever
whatevs - whatever
whats ^ - whats up
what^ - what's up?
whenevs - whenever
whevah - where ever
whever - whatever
whf - Wanna have fun?
whit - with
whodi - friend
whr - where
whs - wanna have sex
wht - What
whteva - what ever
whteve - whatever
whtever - whatever
whtevr - whatever
whtvr - whatever
wht^ - what up
whubu2 - what have you been up to
whubut - what have you been up to
whut - what
whyb - where have you been
whyd - What Have You Done
wid - with
widout - without
wieu2 - What Is Everyone Up To
wif - With
wiid - what if i did
wilco - will comply
winnar - winner
wio - without
wip - Work In progress

wit - with
witcha - with you
witfp - What is the f**king point
witu - with you
witw - what in the world
witwct - What is the world coming too
witwu - who is there with you
witwwyt - what in the world were you thinking
wiu - What is up?
wiuwu - what is up with you
wiv - **with**
wiw - wife is watching
wiwhu - wish I was holding you
wiwt - wish i was there
wiyp - what is your problem
wjwd - What Jesus Would Do
wk - week
wkd - wicked
wkend - weekend
wl - will
wlc - welcome
wlcb - welcome back
wlcm - welcome
wld - would
wlkd - walked
wlos - wife looking over Shoulder
wltm - would like to meet
wmao - working my a** off
wmd - Weapons Of Ma** Destruction
wmgl - wish me good luck
wml - Wish Me Luck
wmyb - What Makes You Beautiful
wn - when
wna - want to
wnkr - wanker
wnrn - why not right now
wnt - want
wntd - what not to do
woa - word of advice
woc - welcome on cam

wochit - watch it
woe - what on earth
woft - Waste of f**king time
wogge - what on god's green earth?
wogs - waste of good sperm
wolo - we only live once
wombat - waste of money, brains, and time
woot - woohoo
wot - what
wotevs - whatever
wotv - What's on Television?
wotw - word of the week
woum - what's on your mind
wowzers - wow
woz - was
wp - wrong person
wpe - worst president ever (Bush)
wrd - word
wrdo - weirdo
wrgad - who really gives a d**n
wrgaf - Who really gives a f**k?
wrk - work
wrm - which reminds me
wrng - wrong
wrt - with regard to
wrtg - writing
wrthls - Worthless
wru - where are you
wrud - what are you doing
wruf - where are you from
wruu2 - what are you up to
wsb - wanna cyber?
wsf - we should f**k
wshtf - when s**t hits the fan
wsi - why should I
wsibt - when should i be there
wsidi - Why Should I Do It
wsop - world series of poker
wswta - What shall we talk about?
wtb - Want to buy

wtbd - what's the big deal
wtbh - What the bloody hell
wtc - what the crap
wtcf - what the crazy f**k
wtd - what the deuce
wtf - what the f**k
wtfaud - what the f**k are you doing?
wtfay - who the f**k are you
wtfayd - what the f**k are you doing
wtfayt - why the f**k are you talking
wtfayta - What the f**k are you talking about?
wtfb - what the f**k b***h
wtfbs - What the f**k bull s**t
wtfc - Who The f**k Cares
wtfdik - what the f**k do i know
wtfdum - what the f**k do you mean
wtfduw - What the f**k do you want?
wtfdyw - what the f**k do you want
wtfe - What The f**k Ever
wtfever - what the f**k ever
wtfg - What the f**king god
wtfh - what the f**king hell
wtfhb - what the f**king hell b***h
wtfhwt - what the f**king hell was that
wtfigo - what the f**k is going on
wtfigoh - what the f**k is going on here
wtfit - what the f**k is that
wtfits - what the f**k is this s**t
wtfiu - what the f**k is up
wtfiup - what the f**k is your problem
wtfiuwy - what the f**k is up with you
wtfiwwu - what the f**k is wrong with you
wtfiwwy - what the f**k is wrong with you
wtfiyp - what the f**k is your problem
wtfm - what the f**k, mate?
wtfmf - what the f**k mother f**ker
wtfo - what the f**k over
wtfru - what the f**k are you
wtfrud - What the f**k are you doing?
wtfrudng - what the f**k are you doing

wtfrudoin - what the f**k are you doing
wtfruo - what the f**k are you on?
wtfruttd - what the f**k are you trying to do
wtfs - what the f**king s**t?
wtfuah - what the f**k you a**h**e
wtful - What the f**k you loser
wtfwjd - what the f**k would jesus do
wtfwt - what the f**k was that
wtfwtd - what the f**k was that dude
wtfwtf - what the f**k was that for?
wtfya - what the f**k you a**h**e
wtfyb - what the f**k you b***h
wtg - way to go
wtgds - way to go dumb s**t
wtgp - Want to go Private
wth - what the heck
wtharud - what the heck are you doing
wthau - who the hell are you
wthauwf - what the hell are you waiting for
wthay - who the hell are you
wthayd - what the heck are you doing
wthaydwmgf - what the hell are you doing with my girlfriend
wthdydt - why the hell did you do that
wthhyb - where the hell have you been?
wthigo - what the hell is going on
wthiwwu - What the hell is wrong with you
wtho - want to hang out?
wthru - Who the heck are you
wthrud - what the hell are you doing?
wths - want to have sex
wthswm - want to have sex with me
wthwt - what the hell was that?
wthwut - what the hell were you thinking
wthyi - what the hell you idiot
wtii - what time is it
wtiiot - What time is it over there?
wtityb - whatever, tell it to your blog
wtly - Welcome to last year
wtmf - what the mother f**k
wtmfh - what the mother f**king hell

wtmi - way too much information
wtmtr - what's the matter
wtp - where's the party
wtrud - what are you doing
wts - want to sell
wtt - want to trade
wttp - want to trade pictures?
wtv - Whatever
wtva - whatever
wtvr - whatever
wtwm - what time are we meeting?
wtwr - well that was random
wu - what's up
wu - what's up?
wu2kilu - want you to know I love you
wub - love
wubmgf - Will You Be My Girlfriend?
wubu2 - what you been up to
wubut - what you been up too
wud - would
wudev - Whatever
wudn - what you doing now
wugowm - will you go out with me
wula - what you looking at?
wuld - would
wuny - wait until next year
wussup - What is up?
wut - what
wutb - What are you talking about
wutcha - What are you
wuteva - whatever
wutevr - what ever
wuts - what is
wutup - What's Up
wuu2 - what you up too
wuu2 - what you up to
wuu22m - what you up to tomorrow
wuut - what you up to
wuv - love
wuwh - Wish you were here

wuwt - what's up with that
wuwta - what do you want to talk about
wuwtab - what do you want to talk about
wuwtb - what do you want to talk about
wuwtta - what you want to talk about
wuwu - what up with you
wuz - was
wuza - what's up
wuzup - what's up
wwc - who would care
wwcnd - What would Chuck Norris do
wwdhd - What would David Hasselhoff do
wwe - World Wrestling Entertainment
wwgf - when we gonna f**k
wwhw - when where how why
wwikt - why would i know that
wwjd - what would jesus do?
wwt - what was that
wwtf - what was that for
wwudtm - what would you do to me
wwut - what were you thinking
www - world wide web
wwwy - what's wrong with you
wwy - where were you
wwycm - when will you call me
wwyd - what would you do?
wwyd2m - what would you do to me
wwyt - What were you thinking
wy - Why?
wyas - wow you are stupid
wyatb - wish you all the best
wyauimg - Why you all up in my grill?
wybts - were you born this sexy
wyc - will you come
wycm - Will You Call Me
wyd - what are you doing
wyg - will you go
wygac - when you get a chance
wygam - When you get a minute
wygowm - Will you go out with me

wygwm - will you go with me
wyhi - Would You Hit It?
wyhswm - would you have sex with me
wyltk - wouldn't you like to know
wylym - Watch Your Language Young Man
wym - What You Mean?
wyn - What's your name
wyp - what's your problem?
wypsu - will you please shut up
wys - wow you're stupid
wysiayg - what you see is all you get
wysitwirl - what you see is totally worthless in real life
wysiwyg - what you see is what you get
wyw - What You Want
wywh - wish you were here
wywo - while you were out
w\e - whatever
x treme - extreme
xb36t - Xbox 360
xbf - ex-boyfriend
xbl - xbox live
xcept - except
xcpt - except
xd - extreme droll
xellent - excellent
xfer - transfer
xgf - exgirlfriend
xing - crossing
xit - Exit
xl - extra large
xlnt - Excellent
xmas - christmas
xmpl - example
xoac - Christ on a crutch
xor - hacker
xover - crossover
xox - hugs and kisses
xoxo - hugs and kisses
xp - experience
xpect - expect

xplaned - explained
xpt - except
xroads - crossroads
xs - excess
xtc - ecstasy
xtra - extra
xtreme - extreme
xyz - examine your zipper
xyzpdq - Examine Your Zipper Pretty Darn Quick
y - why
y w - you're welcome
y!a - yahoo answers
y'all - you all
y/n - yes or no
y/o - Years Old
y00 - you
y2b - Youtube
y2k - year 2000
ya - yeah
yaaf - you are a f**
yaafm - You Are A f**king Moron
yaagf - you are a good friend
yaai - You are an idiot
yaf - you're a f**
yafi - you're a f**king idiot
yag - you are gay
yall - you all
yapa - yet another pointless acronym
yaqw - You are quite welcome
yarly - yeah really
yas - you are stupid
yasan - You are such a nerd
yasf - you are so funny
yasfg - you are so f**king gay
yasg - you are so gay
yasw - you are so weird
yatb - you are the best
yatwl - you are the weakest link
yaw - you are welcome
yayo - cocaine

ybbg - Your Brother By Grace
ybs - you'll be sorry
ybya - you bet your a**
ycliu - You could look it up
ycmtsu - You Can't Make This s**t Up
ycntu - Why Cant You?
yctwuw - you can think what you want
ydpos - you dumb piece of s**t
ydtm - You're dead to me
ydufc - Why do f**king care?
yduwtk - why do you want to know
ye - yeah
yea - yeah
yer - you're
yermom - your mother
yesh - yes
yew - you
yfb - you f**king b*****d
yfg - you're f**king gay
yfi - you f**king idiot
ygg - you go girl
ygm - You Got Mail
ygp - you got punked!
ygpm - you've got a private message
ygrr - you got rick rolled
ygtbfkm - you've got to be f**king kidding me
ygtbk - you've got to be kidding
ygtbkm - you got to be kidding me
ygtbsm - You've got to be shitting me
ygtsr - you got that s**t right
yh - yeah
yhbt - you've been trolled
yhew - you
yhf - you have failed
yhgtbsm - You Have Got To Be Shitting Me
yhl - you have lost
yhm - You have mail
yhpm - you have a private messge
yhtbt - You Had To Be There
yid - yes, I do

yim - yahoo instant messenger
yiwtgo - Yes, I want to go private
yk - you kidding
yki - You know it
ykisa - Your knight in shining armor
ykm - You're killing me
ykn - you know nothing
ykw - You Know What
ykwim - you know what I mean
ykwya - you know who you are
ykywywm - you know you wish you were me
ylb - you little b***h
ym - your mom
ymbkm - you must be kidding me
yme - why me
ymfp - Your Most Favorite Person
ymg2c - your mom goes to college
ymgtc - Your Mom Goes To college
ymiaw - your mom is a w***e
ymislidi - you make it sound like i did it
ymmd - You Made My Day
ymmv - your mileage may vary
ymrasu - Yes, My Retarded a** Signed Up
yn - why not
yng - young
ynk - you never know
ynm - yes, no, maybe
ynt - why not
ynw - you know what
yo - year old
yo' - your
yodo - you only die once
yolo - you only live once
yolt - you only live twice
yomank - you owe me a new keyboard
yooh - you
yor - your
youngin - young person
yoy - why oh why
ypmf - you pissed me off

ypmo - you piss me off
ypom - your place or mine
yqw - you're quite welcome
yr - year
yrbk - Yearbook
yrms - You Rock My Socks
yrs - years
yrsaf - You Are Such A Fool
yrsm - you really scare me
yrss - you are so sexy
yru - why are you?
yrubm - why are you bugging me?
yrusm - Why are you so mean
ys - you suck
ysa - You Suck a**
ysal - you suck at life
ysati - you suck at the internet
ysf - you stupid f**k
ysic - why should I care
ysitm - your shirt is too small
ysm - you scare me
ysoab - You son of a b***h
yss - you stupid s**t
yswnt - why sleep when not tired?
yt - You there?
ytd - year to date
ytf - why the f**k
ytfwudt - why the f**k would you do that?
ythwudt - Why the hell would you do that
ytis - You think I'm special?
ytm - you tell me
ytmnd - You're the man now, dog!
yty - why thank you
yu - You
yua - you ugly a**
yuo - you
yup - yes
yur - your
yust - why you say that
yvfw - you're very f**king welcome

yvw - you're very welcome
yw - you're welcome
ywapom - you want a piece of me?
ywia - You're welcome in advance
ywic - why would i care
yws - you want sex
ywsyls - you win some you lose some
ywud - yo whats up dude
ywvm - you're welcome very much
ywywm - you wish you were me
yysw - yeah, yeah, sure, whatever
z'omg - Oh my God
z0mg - oh my god
zex - sex
zh - Zero Hour
zig - cigarette
zomfg - oh my f**king god
zomg - Oh my God
zomgzorrz - oh my god
zoot - woohoo
zot - Zero Tolerance
zt - zoo tycoon
zup - what's up?

BOUNCE ADDISION
GLOSSARY OF JAMAICAN REGGAE-RASTA WORDS,
EXPRESSIONS, AND SLANG.

A

A (ah)- Means many things from: a, to, is, it, the, will, ECT. 'A' is said
before action will or has taken place.
A door (ah do-ah)- Out doors; outside.
A go (ah go)- To go or will go. Mi a go a door. (I am going outside).
Ackee- African fruit introduced in Jamaica in 1778; is Jamaicas national fruit and is the second main ingredient of Jamaica's national dish combination, ackee and saltfish.
Agony (ah-gon-ee)- Sexual orgasm or sensation of sex.
Ah sey one (ah seh won)- Expression to say that something is really cool and great.
Aile (i'll)- Oil.
Aks (ax)- Ask.
A lie- Your lying; that is a lie.
All fruits ripe- Everything is just great. All is good.
All di while- All the time; sometimes; the time during. All the while dem depon di bashment. (They are partying all the time.)
An- (ahn) And.
A nuh mi- Means that that's not me … It's not me to...I am not one to…A nuh mi fi like it. (I am not one to like that).
Aright (ah-rite)- All right, sure, yes, okay.
'At- Hot; also hat.
'At steppa- Hot stepper, a jail breaker and one in trouble with the law.
A true- It is true; I am not lying.

B

Baan- Born. A weh ya baan? (Where were you born?)
Baby madda- Mother of a child.
Babylon (bah-bee-lon)- A Rasta word for the police and the corrupt system.
Backside (bok-side)- Refers to someone else's self, expressed towards another person. A rude way to refer to someone. Move yu backside. (Move your self).

Badda (bad-da)- Bother. Naa Badda mi. (Don't bother me.)
Bad like yaz- Expression for saying something is really cool.
Bad man/bwoy- Criminal type guy. A really bad individual. Bad man no flee. (Gangsters don't run away.)
Bag juice- The cheapest fruit punch money can buy.
Bait (be-it)- Scoundrel, punk, scum, and these types of people. Ooman naa like bait. (Women don't like punks.)
Bald head- A Rasta label for one who is too caught up with the evil
system—Babylon. Also is anyone who is a non-dreadlocks; usually white people.
Bandu- A hair band worn by women.
Bandulu (ban-doo-loo)- criminal; crooked activity; also means a fake
passport/visa.
Bare (beer)- Only. Is bare pickney yahso. (There's only children here.)
Bash, Bashy- This is a popular slang term that means cool, awesome, nice stuff, ECT.
Bashment- A great event or happening; dancehall; party. Also the same as bashy above. Dem bashment gyal. (They are girls who like to party.). Wi gwaan hab a bashment time. (We are going to have a great time.) Batty- Primarily means butt; also signals to homosexuals. 'Im a battyman. (He is gay).
Beg- To ask; also means to beg. Di man dem beg fa jooks. (The men beg
for sex.)
Big up- This is a popular term for saying what's up and a gesture of tribute. Big up uno dem. (Praise to all of them).
Bill- A basic Jamaican $100 bill. Worth just over two U.S. dollars.
Blessed- A Rasta word; blessing(s).
Bling- Flashy and expensive; necklace or chain. Look pon mi bling. (Look at my chain).
Bloodclot- Strong curse word.
Bloodfire (blud-fiah)- Hell.
Blouse an skirts- Politcally correct version of the curse word bumboclot.
Bly- Favor or chance. Mi mus get a bly. (I must get a chance.) Usually referring to driving on the road.
Bobo dread- A certain sect of Rastas that wear turbans and carry

brooms to signify cleansiness. They are of the Bobo Shanti order and are true followers of Prince Emmanuel.
Bodderation (bod-da-ray-shun)- A comical version of "Bother."
Bokkle (bok-el)- Bottle.
Boots- Condoms; also shoes.
Bout- About. Naa worry bout it. (Don't worry about it).
Bow- to perform oral sex; mostly on a woman.
Box- To fight and punch. She box 'im face. (She punched his face.)
Bredda- Brother.
Bredren- Fellow friends and collegues; brothers in unity.
Browning- Complementing a black person of light skin, and good complexion.
Bruk- Broke, broken, break. Nuh bruk it. (Don't break it).
Brukout- A climax of pure energy and excitement; to act unruly. Usually at a party.
Buck- To accidentally bump into; to meet by chance.
Bud- Bird.
Buddy- Male genital.
Bulla- Cake.
Bumboclot- King of curse words.
Bun- To get cheated on; also burn, kill, and to smoke. She gi 'im bun ka im bun whole heap a herb. (She cheated on him because he smokes a whole heap of herb.) Di Rasta dem say, "Bun dung queer!" (The Rastas say, "Burn down (kill) the queers!")
Bupps- Financially providing for a woman. She bupps im out. 'Im her bupps. (She played him for money. He is her sugar daddy).
Bush weed- A term for rendering poor quality herb.
Buss- To bust; like to bust a move; burst out; unruly.
Bwoy (b-why)- Boy. This is a common term for anybody — male or female.

C
Ca (cah)- Because. Also can be the word "Can". Mi ca hab…? (Can I have…?)
Card- To play a joke or trick. Dem play a card pon mi. (They tricked me).
Cargo- A big and heavy gold or expensive chain one wears to show wealth.
Casco (kas-ko)- Imitation, fake designer clothes.
Cat- Female genitals. Mi nuh like fi bowcat. (I don't like to perform

oral sex).
Chaka-chaka- Messy and untidy.
Cha/cho- Expression of surprise. Cha! (What!)
Champion- A person who is extraordinary on the dancefloor and in the bed.
Chalice- The Rasta water bong/pipe that is made from a hollowed coconut.
Chatty-Chatty- Overly talkative to the point of irritation.
Check it deep- Check it out. When mi check it deep, a casco name brand. (When I checked it out, it was a fake).
Chewsday- Tuesday.
Chi chi- Gay, homosexual, queer. Chi-chi man. (Gay man.)
Chuck- Full-size truck.
Clean- Sexual expression for giving a blowjob.
Cock it up- Aggressive sex.
Coil- Term for money when dollars are wrapped in a roll.
Coppa- Copper; a term for a coin valued less than a dollar.
Coo- Look. Coo yah! (Look here!)
Coolie- Jamaican Indian from India.
Coolie hair- Straight hair.
Craven- Greedy. Craven choke puppy. This is a famous line that depicts someone who wants everything but, when they get it, they can't handle it.
Cris- Slang for cool and instyle. Dat cris. (That is cool.)
Crosses- Problems and misfortunes. Mi always inna crosses. (I always have bad luck.)
Culture (kul-cha)- Reflecting or pertaining to the roots, values and traditions of Rastas.
Cuss-cuss- Shouting fight with bad words.
Cutchie- A clay-fired earth piece that fits into a chalice needed to hold ganja; a cup.
Cutlass- A cutting instrument; a very large knife.
Cutta- Cutter; can opener; cutting tool.
Cut yeye- Cutting your eye at someone by turning the eyes the other way.
Cyar (key-ar)- Car.

D

Dan- Than
Dandimite- Dynamite
Darkers (dah-kahs)- Sunglasses, shades.
Dat- That
Dawta (doh-ta)- Daughter; woman, good woman friend.
Dead- Dead, die, killed, to kill. 'Im a dead. (He is dead).
Dear- Expensive. Dat cost dear. (That is very expensive.)
Deestant (dee-stant)- Decent.
Dege-dege (deh-geh deh-geh)- Measly or skimpy.
Deh- There — as in place. Also asks where something is. Weh ih deh? (Where is it?)
Deh 'bout- Nearby, close to.
Dehya (deh-yah)- Here or there.
Dem- Them. Use dem after plural objects. Di gal dem. (The girls.)
Depan (deh-pon)- On; on top of; upon.
Des- Desperate. Im sey im des fi a food. (He said he's desperate for food).
Dey (dayah)- They; there, as in to be or exist. Dey nuh odda way. (There is no other way). Nuh milk nuh dey. (There is no milk there). Dey say. (They say.)
Di- The; did, was. 'Im did dun di ting? (Did he complete the thing?)
Dideh (di-dayah)- Was there or right over there. 'Im dideh. (He is/was there). Member when wi dideh?
Dis- This.
Disya- This right here.
Don- A term and name for one who is well respected.
Doondoos (dune-deuce)- Referring to an albino.
Downpress- Rasta word for "Oppress".
Dread- Person who has dreadlocks, greeting to friend, expression of a good idea.
Dreadnut- Rasta word for "Coconut."
Drop legs- To dance.
Dub- Mixed music of electronicreggae.
Dun- Done, finished, over with; kill. Mi dun feel bad. (I am done feeling bad). Mi dun dweet. (I have finished doing it).
Dun know- Don't know.
Dung- Down. Come dung. Sidung (Come down. Sit down.)
Duppy (dup-pee)- Ghost.

Dutty- Dirty; also a popular slang expression, as in Dutty yo.
Dutty gal- Tin mackerel. This is common food for the poor.
Dween- Doing.
Dweet- Do it.

E

Ease-up- To relax. Ease up uno self. (Relax yourselves.)
Eat unda sheet- Expression of performing oral sex.
Eaz haad- Ears hard. Means stubbornness or thickskulled; one who
doesn't listen. Yu rass claat haad eaz. (You are damn stubborn.)
Eff- If
Ends- A place. Mi a go pon one ends still. (I am going to one place).
Eveling- Evening
Everything cook and curry- Everything is just fine.

F

Fa- For. Wa mek yu dweet fa? (Why did you do it for?)
Faas- Fast. Tap drive faas. (Stop driving fast).
Facety (fe-ast-ee)- Bad mannered and nasty; acting fresh.
Fambly- Family.
Fass- Nosey.
Favor (fa-va)- Looks like; resembles. 'Im a fava a dinna pig. (He resembles the size of a pig.) She fava har mudda. (She looks like her mother.)
Feel no way- Not taken in offense; not to worry or care.
Fi (fee)- To. This is the main Jamaican prepostion. Mi naa waan fi do it. (I don't want to do it).
Fi mi, fi she, fi yu, fi 'Im- Mine, hers, yours, his. Shows possession. A fi mi cyar. (My car). Fi dem. (Theirs.)
Fiah (fi-ah)- Fire; also used to designate the smoking of ganja. More fiah! (More weed!)
Fit- when used of fruits and vegetables, it means that fruit is ready to pick and is fully grown, though not necessarily fully ripe to eat.
Flim- Film; mostly camera film. Mi need fi buy flim becaa' no flim in'ai camra. (I need to buy film because there is no film in the camera.)
Flex- To chill and hang out having a time; to plan an activity.

Follow- To travel close to, to follow or seek. Follow back a mi. (Follow me.) Di fly a follow yu head. (The fly is seeking your head.)
Foot- Any part of the entire leg. 'Im foot a bruk means that his leg is broken.
Forward- Future; to go or to move.
Fren'- Friend.
Frock- Dress. Also an expression, e.g. Fit 'n frock means everything is good.
Fram- From; since. Mi dehya fram 6:00. (I have been here since 6:00). Fram when mi a pickney mi a dweet. (I have been doing it since I was a kid).
Fresh- Not ready; still bitter or sour. Di juice a fresh still. (The juice is still raw tasting.)
Fuckery (fuk-ree)- A maljustice, something wrong and unfair; this is not considered a bad word. A fuckery dat. (That was a messed up thing).

G

Gaan- Literally means gone. 'Im gaan. (He is gone.)
Gaan to bed- An expression of loving something very much.
'Gainst- Against. She fight 'gainst mi. (She fought against me.)
Galang- Go along.
Ganja- Marijuana.
Gansey- T-shirt.
Gates- Home. Many homes in JA have gates. One's "gates" is one's home.
Get- To have, to have had, got, gotten. Mi get fi realize. (I realize or I have realized.)
General- A cool and smooth operator.
Ginnal- Trickster, con-person. 'Im so ginnal. (He is a tricky person.)
Ginnygog- An influential person--derogative.
Gimme- Give me.
Give tanks- A expression of gratitude; a Rasta expression.
Glamity- Womans' sexual private area.
Gleena- Newspaper; the Jamaican Gleener.
Godeh- Go there. Mi no go deh. (I'm not going there)
Gone- Gone, passed, left. Mi see har di Monday gone. (I saw her the passed Monday.)

Gorgon- Outstanding person and very well respected. 'Im a don gorgon. (He is a master of situations).
Greetings- An opening greeting used heavily by Rastas.
Grindsman- One who is great in bed.
Grow- To raise. She grow mi. (She raised me.)
Gwaan- Go on. Wa a gwaan? (What's going on?)
Gwine (gween)- Going. Wi gwine adoor. (We are going outside.)
Gweh- Go away.

H

Hab- Have
Haffi- Have to.
Half eediat (af ee-dee-at)- A very stupid person.
Hanga- Closet; hanger.
Hangle- Handle.
Har- Her
Haste (hee-ase)- To be in a hurry. Mek haste. (Hurry up)
Hat- Hurt
Higgla- A street vendor; comes from the British word higgler.
Hol ih dung- Hold it down. Means keep it steady; make a secret; not to be told.
Honor (hon-nah)- A Rasta word; greeting or good-bye.
Hose- Penis. Mi kyaan lock mi hose off. (I can't keep it in side; in this
case the speaker is stating being excessively sexually active.)
Hot steppa- Hot stepper, which is a criminal; fugitive; escapee from jail.
Hush- Sorry. [Person 1] Ouch! Yu hut mi! [Person 2] Hush. {1} You hurt me!

I

I an I- Rasta speech for me. Me, myself, and I.
I-cense- Rasta word for ganga, which is taken from the Biblical word "Incense."
I-ditate- Rasta word for "Meditate."
I-dren- Rasta word for bredren, which is taken from the Biblical word "Brethren."
I-laloo- Rasta word for "Callaloo", which is spinach.
I-man / I-mon - Refers to the self. I-man waan dat. (I want that). Rasta for: Me or you.

I-ney- A classic Rasta greeting.
I-ree- Rasta word for "Irie", which means to be happy.
I-sire- Rasta word for "Desire"
I-tal- Rasta term for "Vital", which is a strict diet and way of life. Most commonly Rasta food that is pure, unprocessed, and unsalted.
I-tes- Rasta word for "Heights." The I-tes color for the Rasta is Red. This word is also used as a greeting.
I-wah- Rasta word for "Hour."
I-yah- Me (I) or you.
Ih (ih or ee)- It. Weh ih deh? (Where is it?)
'Im- Him
Informa- (in-fah-mah)Informer. One who narcs or tells on others-- usually to the police. Informers are not respected.
Inna- In the. This word can also be spelled with only one 'n'.
Inna di lights- Expression to say tomorrow. See you inna di lights. (See you tomorrow.)
Irie (I-ree)- Means everything is alright. Expression of feeling great and cool.
Iron bird (Irun-buud)- An Iron bird is an airplane. Yu jus come off di ironbud. (You've just come off the plane.)?)

J
Ja, Jamdown, Jamdung- Words for Jamaica.
Jacket- Bastard; a child that is raised by another father. (Usually from the wife cheating on someone else and the father never knowing.)
Jah- Lord. Jah Bless. (God Bless.)
Jah guide- A Rasta farewell and good-bye. Literally says that "God shall guide."
Jah know- Lord or God knows; an expression of agreement.
Jake, Johnny, Joe- Terms Jamaicans use to yell and call out when they see white Americans. Hey Jake!
Jancro- John Crow, which is the name for the hated albino buzzard/vulture; also an expression of hate.
Jesum Piece- A soft expresson of aggrivation.
Jester- To joke; kidding. Mi naa jesta. (I'm not kidding.)
Jook- To pierce or poke; to have sex.
Jus begin fi dead- Expression saying that people were really shocked or amazed, like they could have dropped dead. Dem jus

begin fi dead when wi did wi ting. (They almost dropped dead when we did our thing).

K

Ketch- To ketch; to get, to achieve.
Key- Slang for good friend. Similar to "My main man." Wa'ppun mi key? (What's up man?) This word also means the normal key we are used to for opening doors.
Kill mi dead- Expression of certainty; I'll do it at all costs, no matter what. Mi muss a go kill mi dead. (I'll get there no matter what.)
Kiss teet- A facial expression when the lips are pressed together kissing and the eyebrows up. Makes a hiss. Also is a very rude jesture and sound of the face and mouth.
Ku- Look. Ku pon dis. (Look at this).
Kya (Key-a) Care. Mi nuh kya. (I don't care.)
Kyaan- Can't; can not. Note: some spellings have it as "Cyaan" or "Caan".
Kyaan done- Can't finish; never ending. Mi lub yu kyaan done. (My love for you can't end.)
Kyarri (key-ah-ree)- Carry.

L

Laas- Last; or lose.
Labba-Labba- Talking to much. Labba mout. (A chatter mouth.)
Lambsbread- A Rasta term for high-grade ganja.
Lang- Long. Lang time mi a wait. (I've waited for a long time.)
Large (laaj)- Very well respected. Dat large. (That's popular). Also used as a slang term, "Large up!" (Similar to "Big up" — a term of fond greeting and appreciation.)
Lef- Leave, left, passed.
Leggo- To let go; leave, let's go. She leggo har numba. (She gave out her number.)
Legsus- A spoof on the luxury car, Lexus, but expresses the walking
power of the legs.
Liad (li-ad)- Liar. Yu a liad. (You are a liar).
Lickle- Little.
Lickle more- A saying of goodbye.

Light- Power; electricity.
Likky-Likky- One who is greedy about eating everything seen. Yu too
likky-likky.
Lilly- Little, tiny.
Link up- Slang for "Hooking up"; getting or meeting together, ect. Mi link yu up layta. (I'll get with you later.)
Lock up- Closed. Di store dem a lock up. (The stores are closed).

M

Machet- A machete.
Maga- Skinny and slender.
Man juice- Sperm.
Manley- A Jamaican $1000 bill that has former prime minister Michael
Manley.
Mantell- Male gigolo; a real player and whore of a man.
Marina- A sleeveless wifebeater T-shirt, commonly netted.
Mas- An old and wise master; a old-timer who deserves respect.
Mascot- Someone who is lame, inferior; can mean gay.
Mash it up- Expression of doing well; like, "Break a leg"; be a big success.
Mek- Let; make. Mek wi dweet. (Let us do it). Mek up yu mind. (Make up your mind). Dat di best eva mek. (That's the best ever made.)
Memba- Remember.
Mi- Me, I, mine. Mi soon come. (I'll be there soon). [Can be pronounced
Mee or Meh]
Mon- Perhaps the single most important Jamaican word, "Mon" can represent every person in Jamaica — man, woman, and child. Yes mon! (Yes man, woman, or child!)
'Mongst- Amongst
More time- Popular expression for saying good-bye. This must be said with power and voice. More time! (Later!)
Mos def- Most definitely. An expression meaning, of course, yes, sure, ECT.
Mr. Mention- A real ladies man who is the talk of the town so to speak.
Mudda- Mother.

Muss- Must.
Mussi- Must be.
My yute- My youth. Friendly expression of calling a friend or youger vone. Hey my yute. (Hey my friend).

N
Naa- A variation of the word No.
Nanny- A Jamaican $500 bill worth about 11 U.S. dollars.
Neba- Never
Negga (neh-gah)- Negro. See Nyega.
Neegle- needle.
Neegle yeye- literally means "Needle's eye". Has reference to something very small. Also refers to the female sexual organ.
Nize (niz)- Noise
Nuff- Plenty, too much, many, tons, a lot, ECT.
Nuh- No, now, or know.
Nuh true?- Expression of verifying the truth; Isn't it so?
Nuh easy- A very popular expression saying one is acting a bit off the wall or uneasy, or when ones manners are not in order. Yu nuh easy! Nutten- Nothen.
Nyabinghi- The traditional and orthodox Rastafarian movement of black supremacy and visions of the Ethiopian Zion; a Rasta spiritual gathering with drumming and chanting.
Nyam (nee-ahm)- To eat. Mek wi nyam. (Let's eat.)
Nyami-Nyami- Expression of one who eats too much.
Nyega (nee-yeg-ah)- term for black person; nigger. Dutty Nyega. (Poor and trashy person—same as white trash in the U.S.) White nyega. (Jamaican born white person.)

O
Obeah- The withcraft or spiritual science native of Africa. It is the type of voodoo in Jamaica. She a put Obeah pon ya. (She cast a spell on you.)
Odda (ud-dah)- Other. Dey nuh odda way. (There's no other way.)
Ongle- Only.
Ooman- Woman.
Ooo- Who. Is fi ooo? (Whose is it?)
Ova- Over.
Ovastan- Rasta word for "Understand". Literally means "Overstand".

P
Pear (peer)- Avocado.
Peas- Beans. Rice an peas. (Rice and beans).
Pickney- Child, children, kids.
Poas- Post; to mail.
Priors- Prayers.
Pull- To open. Pull di can a peas. (Open the can of beans).
Pum, Punash, Punaani- Female genitals.
Pussyclot- Curse word.
Pussyhole (pus-swhol)- Curse word.
Pyur (peer)- Only; used in conjunction with things in large quantities. Always remember to say this like peer. Pure gal waan mi. (Many girls want me).

Q
Quashi- a peasant
Quips- a small portion
Quing-up : to compress
Quattie : of no value, the term is derived from the name that was given to the 1/2 penny that was used in Jamaica during Britsh rule.

R
Radda- Rather.
Ragga- The current name of popular regae music. Ragga music relies
heavily on a digital equipment.
Raggamuffin- A Jamaican ghetto dweller. Naa mess wit no raggamuffin. (Don't mess with a ghetto person.)
Rakstone- Rocks, stones. Rakstone inna mi shoe. (I have rocks in my
shoes.)
Rass/Raas (rass/rahz)- Common word and expression meaning ass; also it can add intensity to objects or basic words in normal speech. Ending a word with clot makes it a curse word.
Ray Ray- This is a term used when someone is talking too much or telling a story. Similar to saying blah blah.
Ready- A person, usually always a woman, who is sexually attractive.
Red- High or drunk. Also is the color of a person who is not fully

Black. E.g. Red Rat.
Red yeye- One who is covetous and jelous of things. Yu yeye too red.
Reespek- Respect. A very popular Rasta greeting that shows courtesy.
Renk- Foul; smelling bad; very rude.
Response- Responsible. Response fi ooo? (Responsible for whom?)
Rest- To relax and settle down. Rest mon! (Calm down!)
Rhaatid (rah-tid)- A mild exclamation of surprise or irritation. Similar to gosh, heck, and damn.
Righted- Correct and with sense. Dat nuh righted. (That was with out sense).
Rockas- Music to "rock" to. Slang for music and enjoying such.
Romp- To mess with or play. Yu wanna romp wit me? (Do you want to mess with me?)
Rope een- To join in or come in on an activity going on.
Rude bwoy (rood bwhy)- A basic slang term. Can be a common greeting to a cool friend or it can describe a tough guy, rebel, or criminal. Wa'ppun rude bwoy? (What's up man?) 'Im run di rude bwoy bizness. (He runs the criminal business).
Run a boat- A saying where many people will cook and eat a big dinner.

S
Sa (sah)- Sir.
Salt (saál)- Bad luck, unlucky. Mi get salt. (I was unlucky.)
Samfi (sam-fi)- A trickster and conman out to get money. 'Im a samfi man. (He is a conman).
Sapps- A man who is controlled by a woman.
Satday, Satnight- Saturday and Saturday night.
Sciecne- A term for the following of the Obeah witchcraft cult practice. She a scientist becaa she follow di Science people dem. (She is an occult practitioner [Obeah] because she follows people of that cult.)
Scenty (sent-tee)- Smelling good; a good scent. Mi put mi turn on perfume an mi scenty. (I put on my "Turn on" perfume [turns on the woman] and I smell good.)
Screw- To be angry. Screw face. (An angry face.)
See it - Slang for "Do you understand or do you see".
Shorty- This is a slang expression similar to saying 'chick' or girl.

Shot- To shoot, shot, to have been shot. Dem shot 'im dead. (They shot him dead.)
Sidung- Sit down.
Sight- A Rasta term for, "Do you SEE or UNDERSTAND?"
Sistren- A reference or greeting to a group of women — usually formal; sistren are the opposite of "bredren or bredrin". Hi sistren! (Hi ladies!)
Si'ting (si-tin)- Something; a thing that you don't feel like calling the
proper name. Mi a go get dat sinting. (I am going to get that thing).
Skettle- A ho girl or slut; also means anything really cheap. A skettle name brand dat. (Those are cheap brand clothes.) Sket is a shortened version; also a cheap boxed drink.
Skin teet- Smile. Check yu'self befo yu skin ya teet. Check yourself befor you smile.
Slam/Slap- Slang words for sex.
Slump- The slums or ghetto. Dis a di slump. (This is the slum.)
So- Like that; such as that, like such, ECT. This is just a common expression used to decribed anything. Almost always comes at the end of the sentence. Wa mek yu galaan so?(Why are you behaving like such?) Wa mek yu sweet so? (Why are you so sweet?)
Soon come- Term used for general replies in saying that one will be back. However, it does not mean necessarily that one will actually come promptly. Mi a soon come. (I'll come soon.)
Spliff- A very large cone-shaped marijuana cigarette.
Speaky-Spokey- This is when a Jamaican tries to speak like an American or Englishman.
Stamina- Sexual endurance. Di ooman dem wanna stamina daddy, ya
hear. (Women want a man with pleanty of sexual endurance.)
Star- To sport something or an event in style; also slang for "Man".
Stay- To leave alone or let be; to wait; the way someone is. Mek it stay. (Let it be.) Jus stay deh.
Step- To leave. Mi step out yah. (I am leaving now.)
Stoosh- Any person that is rich; a rich object. Dis computa stoosh! (This computer is "stoosh"!) Mi live inna stoosh place. (I live in a rich place.)
Strong money- Just a saying to denote the superiority of American money.
Su-Su (sue-sue)- To gossip and spread rumors. The sound of

whispering in one's ear denotes gossip and backbiting.
Sufferation (suf-fa-ray-shun)- Major suffering, poverty, and trials. A pyur sufferation inna gwaan inna di ghetto.
Sum'ady- Somebody.
Sup'm (sup-hm)- Another way of saying "Something".
Swaaty- Fatty.

T

Tack- Bullet.
Tall- Long. Har hair tall, ee? (Her hair is long, huh?)
Tallowah- Strong and sturdy.
Tam- A large oval-shaped Rasta hat used to cover dreadlocks.
Tan- Stand, stay, wait and see; also to be as in to be such a way. Tandeh. (Stay there, just you wait).
Tanks- Thanks.
Tan pon it lang- Expression of having sex for a long time.
Ten toe turbo- An funny expression meaning to walk and use your feet. It must be known that the majority of Jamaicans walk for transportation.
Teet- Teeth.
Teif- Thief; to steal. Di teif a teif mi tings. (The thief has stolen my things.)
Tek- Take or get. Tek time. (Take time / slow down).
Tess- Test. Yu waan tess mi? (Do you want to test me?)
Trash an ready- A popular slang expression meaning to be very stylish and fashionable.
Tree- Tree; also the number three. 'Im a tree bunna. (He cheats "burns" on three women.)
Truu- Truth; true; through; threw.
Truss mi- Trust me. This is an ever-popular expression used when agreeing with some one. Basically means: "Oh yeh, believe me, I know", ect.
Truut- Truth past tense. 'Im tol di trut. (He told the truth.)
Tun- Turn. Im tun deh. (He turned there).

U

Unda gal pickney- Expression for what is "Under the girls' pants".
Undastan (un-dah-staan)- Understand.
Uno or unno (uh-no)- The plural form of you, you all, the all of you, ECT. Also means all. Uno yu. (All of you.)

Upful- Positive feelings. Yu so upful. (You are cheerful.)
Usband- Husband.

V

Van- Pick-up truck.
Vank- To beat, eliminate, or conquer. Comes from the word vanquish.
Version (ver-shun)- Version; popularly an instrumental version.
Vex- This the key word that is used to mean angry, mad, upset, furious, ECT. Naa mek mi vex, mon! (Don't make me mad!)

W

Wa (wah)- What.
Wa day- The other day. Memba wa day weh wi dweet? (Do you remember the other day when we did it?)
Wa mek? - Why
Waan- Want; need.
Wanga gut- One who has a fat stomach; one who likes to eat and seems hungry all the time; a hungry-belly.
Wa'ppun- What's happening? This is the most popular greeting used.
Always say this instead of the American, "What's up."
Weh- Where; past tense of was; present tense of is; that is.
Wear- To wear; it is worn, worn, wears. Batty ridas still a wear by di gal dem. (Short shorts are still worn by the girls.)
Wheels- Car.
Whole heap- Slang for very large quantities; a lot, a whole heap. Very common to use.
Wi- We, us, our, ours. Naa touch wi tings. (Don't touch our things).
Wicked- Slang for bad or evil. Dat wicked, nuh? (That's cool, huh?)
Winji- Very thin and unattractive. She too winji. (She's too thin.)
Wit- With.
Wrap up- Slang for kidding or joking. Mi naa wrap up. (I am not joking.)
Wood- Penis.
Work (wuk)- Slang for sex.
Wutless- Worthless. When used in conjunction with a man it means one who is lousy in bed.

X

X amount- Countless; many. Mi get x amount a lovin. (I receive plenty of love/sex.)

Y

Ya, Yah- You, here, also can mean yes.
Yahso- Over here; right here.
Ya nuh see it? - Slang for, you know?
Yaad- Yard, place of residence, house, home. Tek mi a mi yaad. (Take me home.) Mi baan a Jamaican Yardi. (I was born a Jamaican.)
Yeh- Yes.
Yeye (yi)- Eye.
Yeyewata- To shed tears, cry.
Yuut- Youth. A popular name for calling a friend; can also refer to someone younger. Also popular using man as ending.

Z

Zed- The letter Z. Fram A to Zed. (From A to Z).
Zeen- Understand, you know, you see, okay, yeh, ECT. One of the most
Zion- This is the holy land talked about the Rastas, which is in Ethiopia.

Lightning Source UK Ltd.
Milton Keynes UK
UKHW041614291018
331393UK00011B/706/P